Magic Guidebooks

Universal Studios

Orlando Florida

2024

FAST AND INFORMATIVE VACATION PLANNING!

Insider Secrets, Hotel & Dining Reviews, and Tips for Universal Studios Florida, Islands of Adventure, The Wizarding World of Harry Potter, Volcano Bay, CityWalk, & More!

ISBN: 979-8-9889768-1-3

Magic Guidebooks

Universal Orlando 2024

- **Amazing Tips for Saving Money and Time** – Fast and useful insider tips and recommendations for saving you money and time planning your trip!
- **Covers All of Universal Orlando** – Including Universal Studios Florida, Universal's Islands of Adventure, Universal's Volcano Bay Water Park, and Universal CityWalk
- **Dedicated Harry Potter Chapter** – The Wizarding World of Harry Potter in detail! Learn the best tips for experiencing the magic!
- **Updated with New Attractions** – Wait less for hot newer rides like the Illumination's Villain-Con Minion Blast, Jurassic World VelociCoaster and Hagrid's Magical Creatures Motorbike Adventure
- **No Express Pass Needed** – Our pre-planned ride lists help fit all of the fun in without the need of buying Express Pass
- **An Honest Approach** – We give you unfiltered ride, restaurant, and hotel reviews with recommendations based on your interests

Table of Contents

INTRODUCTION

ABOUT THIS GUIDE

When developing and writing this book, we had *you* in mind. Maybe you're a first-time visitor to the Universal Orlando Resort, or perhaps you've frequented it over the years. Wherever you come from and whatever your experience, we wanted to provide a complete guide from start to finish, while giving a critique of the Universal Orlando Resort. The purpose of this guide is to provide *real* advice covering the many attractions, restaurants, and hotels from the Resort and beyond.

Who are we? Well, we're theme park enthusiasts who spend a lot of time gathering first-hand knowledge and experiences from all around the world. We've written guidebooks for Disneyland and Walt Disney World—and now we're tackling the fun of the Universal Studios Orlando Resort! Advice from this guide is crafted from our trial, error, and gathered knowledge—and now we're passing the fruit of our hard work on to you!

Keep in mind that this guide is an "unofficial edition," meaning that we are an independent company from Universal and its parent company. We are simply theme park enthusiasts who are giving an honest opinion on what the Resort has to offer. Though we call ourselves "fans" and do our best to keep a fun feel, we're also critical of the Resort when necessary. Overall, we want this guide to be fun, fast, and informative!

FOR UNIVERSAL NEWBIES

If you've never been to the Universal Orlando Resort before, this book is perfect for you! We've crammed our guide with tidbits about the best food, attraction recommendations, hotel pros/cons, and so much more. We'll fill you in on the Resort's lingo, history, and even its future. In the end, you'll have the knowledge of a pro!

FOR RETURN VISITORS

The Universal Orlando Resort is a constantly changing place. From exciting themed dining to upcoming thrilling attractions, *anything* could happen next! If you haven't been to Universal Orlando in ten years, this guide is a great fit.

However, if you visit every week, you probably won't learn much. That, of course, doesn't mean that you won't learn *anything*—but you're likely already a pro and a guide to a place that's essentially your second home won't be much use. Still, if you're curious, we welcome you along for the ride! Even as often as we go, we still learned *a lot* from researching for this book. Also, if you've read our Walt Disney World guide, this book may sound a bit repetitive. A lot of information in this guide is available (almost word-for-word) in our WDW version. However, this guide goes into much more detail!

A WORD FOR ALL

Since Universal Orlando updates so frequently, some of the items in this guide will change even weeks after its publication. Restaurants in CityWalk might close, attractions may be re-themed, popular food items could become discontinued... While most of this content should remain applicable to your trip, we just like to give you a heads up in case you notice a menu item change or an attraction closed for refurbishment.

A BRIEF HISTORY

In 1986, after the success of Universal Studios Hollywood and Walt Disney World, Universal broke ground on a new world-class theme park. Taking advantage of Florida's warm, tropical weather and abundance of land, the movie studio—along with co-founder, Steven Spielberg—began designing attractions for a new set of tourists. While its Hollywood sister park invited guests inside actual film studios, Universal Studios Florida would focus on "riding the movies."

Universal's new, exciting theme park brought guests into the treacherous waters of the movie *Jaws*, the past with *Back to the Future*: *The Ride*, and even to E.T.'s home planet. Keeping with its slogan of "Ride the Movies," Universal Orlando bases many of its attractions on 3-D motion simulators and live entertainment shows based on popular films. Currently, *Transformers: The Ride*, *Despicable Me: Minion Mayhem*, and *The Simpsons Ride* all use motion simulation with enormous screens and automated moving seats to propel guests into storylines. However, Universal also has classic rollercoasters with *Hollywood Rip Ride Rockit* and *Revenge of the Mummy*.

With usually around 10 million visitors a year, Universal Studios Florida is one of the most visited theme parks in the world. With more rides and space than its Hollywood predecessor, Florida's version is an exciting and unforgettable time for movie and thrill ride lovers.

ISLANDS OF ADVENTURE HISTORY

Universal Studios Florida continued its legacy of world-class entertainment when it broke ground in May 1999 with Islands of Adventure. This theme park is comprised of eight "islands" placed across a massive lagoon. Every island is captivating and themed from popular franchises like *Harry Potter*, *Jurassic Park*, Marvel Comics, and Dr. Seuss. While Universal Studios Florida immerses guests in a Hollywood backlot, Islands of Adventure brings fictional worlds to life. Jurassic Park Island is filled with palm trees and dinos, while Hogsmeade Village plunges guests into the magical, snow-covered world of *Harry Potter*.

With its perfect attention to detail, Islands of Adventure feels more like a concretely themed world than an amusement park. Waterfalls, foliage, and well-crafted rides bring both wonder and thrills to its visitors. Young kids will love the colorful and slow-paced world of Seuss Landing, while thrill-riders will seek out Marvel Island's looping Hulk coaster.

Don't worry *Harry Potter* fans, we haven't left you out! Hogsmeade Village is the magical destination you've been searching for your entire life. With sweet Butterbeer carts, working wands, magical gift shops, and even a chance to enter Hogwarts Castle, you might spend half of your day in Hogsmeade, never wishing to return home!

If you haven't figured it out by now, we absolutely love Universal's Islands of Adventure. While it pulls in about a million fewer visitors than Universal Studios, it's by far the better park. Even though we love Universal Studios, too, Islands brings theme park immersion to a new level.

WHICH PARK SHOULD I VISIT?

If you can't decide which park to visit, why not both? If you purchase a park-to-park ticket, you can take the bonus ride, the Hogwarts Express, which connects the two theme parks by a gentle and fun train ride. Both parks have *Harry Potter*-themed attractions, with Hogsmeade Village in Islands of Adventure and Diagon Alley in Universal Studios Florida.

Though Hogsmeade is stunning and home to a few more attractions, Diagon Alley is somehow even more breathtaking. You'll magically enter the area (we won't tell you how—it's a surprise for when you get there) and visit shops, dark back alleys, and even the goblin-run Gringotts bank! The centerpiece of Diagon Alley is a life-size fire-breathing dragon. Yes, *real* fire!

If you haven't already realized, there's a lot to cover before your visit. From *Harry Potter* to Universal CityWalk to Volcano Bay (which we haven't even mentioned yet), this guide covers insider tips and reviews for one of the greatest theme park resorts in the world: Universal Studios Orlando!

WHAT TO EXPECT DURING YOUR VACATION

Orlando, Florida is an ideal location for a theme park because of its year-long sunshine. Likely, as you arrive, you'll see the sun shining with white tufts of cottony clouds. Many times, especially in the late afternoon, it'll be cloudy and gray for an hour or so. Thunderstorms, especially in the summer months, will sweep by and leave as quickly as they came. It's common for it to rain each day in this part of Florida. Fortunately, the rain doesn't last for long. For most of the year, the humidity is high in Central Florida—sometimes even 100% saturating the air. It can feel a bit stifling, but the resorts and parks prepare for this. Air conditioning pumps are in every hotel and indoor ride to help you enjoy your stay.

The parks are large and filled with people happy to enjoy the magic of the movies that Universal brings to life. You'll see visitors from all over the world experiencing attractions with you. Since the Universal theme parks promise more thrills than the Walt Disney World parks, tweens and teens especially love it here.

THE WIZARDING WORLD OF HARRY POTTER

You've never stepped inside of a place like The Wizarding World of Harry Potter. The magic of J. K. Rowling's best-selling book series and record-breaking films transports guests into a real-life wizarding world where it feels like anything can happen! Watch visitors stroll the streets in Hogwarts robes (yes, it's socially acceptable for anyone of any age to dress as a wizard here) and wave their wands to "magically" activate key spots in both parks.

The detailed sets of Hogsmeade Village (Islands of Adventure) and Diagon Alley (Universal Studios Florida) are immersive and instantly captivating. Plus, the delicious treats like a non-alcoholic Butterbeer drink and assortments of magical snacks will have your tastebuds popping (don't worry, adults 21 and older—they have *Harry Potter*-inspired alcoholic beverages, too)! Not only will your photos of The Wizarding World seem unreal, but so will your memories. In fact, there's so much to do in the Wizarding World of Harry Potter that we've dedicated an entire chapter to it!

PHRASES AROUND UNIVERSAL

The Universal Orlando Resort – The area that encompasses all of its theme parks (Universal Studios Florida, Islands of Adventure, and Volcano Bay), the Resort hotels, and the CityWalk entertainment area.

Park-to-Park Ticket – A ticket that allows you to visit two or three of the Universal Orlando parks, as many times as you'd like during that day. To ride the Hogwarts Express train, you will need a Park-to-Park ticket.

Universal Express Pass and Express Pass Unlimited – For an additional cost, you can buy your way to the front of the lines. Express Pass allows one skip per ride in a day, while Express Pass Unlimited allows you to skip as many times as you'd like. If you are staying at a premium Universal Orlando Resort hotel, like the Hard Rock, you will get Express Pass Unlimited included complimentarily during your stay (more on this later).

Single Rider Line – A fast way to get on the rides as long as you don't mind riding without the rest of your party. Not every ride has this feature, but the popular ones often do.

Universal Orlando App – An Apple and Android application that allows you to check wait times, sync a credit card to your ticket or hotel key, and more.

Early Park Admission – If you're staying on property, you can get into the parks an hour early on select days.

Dark Ride – An indoor ride set in a dark building.

Universal Dining Plan – Pre-purchased meal plans to select eateries around the Universal Orlando Resort.

3D – The use of 3D glasses during the ride or attraction.

4D – The use of 3D glasses with added effects like splashing water and rumbling seats.

TapuTapu – A waterproof bracelet used at the Volcano Bay Water Park in order to reserve ride times and more. This device comes with your Volcano Bay admission and you need to return it before leaving the water park (more on this later).

Animatronic – Robotic characters typically used in stage shows and rides.

Halloween Horror Nights (HHN) – A scary, horror-filled takeover of Universal Studios. Walk through mazes filled with actors playing murderers and monsters. This popular event is a secondary ticket price and runs from mid-September to early November.

PHRASES AND WORDS FOR THIS GUIDEBOOK

⋆ **Magic Tips** ⋆ – These are special insider tips and secrets! Magic Tips are designed to:

- Save time waiting in lines
- Get the best viewing areas for shows and parades
- Save money booking
- Plus, many more useful hacks!

RIDE LEVELS

Everyone – Perfect for all ages
Family – Suited for families with kids
Young Kids – Children ages 2-5
Kids – Children ages 6-9
Tweens – Children ages 10-12
Teens – Young people ages 13-17
Adults – People ages 18+

Thrill Riders – Those looking for the maximum thrill. Whether it's a ride with loops like the Hulk Coaster or the high-dropping Doctor Doom's Fearfall, this attraction level is not for the faint of heart.

RESOURCES

General – Visit for booking and reservations: **www.UniversalOrlando.com**

Customer Service – For booking and general questions 1 (407) 363-8000

Our Website – For updates on future copies of our Universal Orlando Resort guidebook: **www.magicguidebooks.com**

CHAPTER ONE
PLANNING YOUR VACATION

PLANNING WHEN TO VISIT

Whether you are choosing dates or already have your vacation slot picked, we cover the day-by-day and month-by-month calendar for Universal. All parks tend to experience the same influxes in vacation demand, so we'll keep it simple and group the entire Resort together. It's important to know the most in-demand dates so that you can plan accordingly to experience the attractions you desire. Rest assured, we have tips for staying ahead of the crowds during your visit!

In this chapter, we will walk you through the choices of travel and our recommendations for saving time and money. Choosing a time for your vacation may not be entirely up to you. It could depend on your work schedule, your previously planned travel dates, or your children's vacation days from school. Whether you have flexible travel dates or not, we have laid out a month-by-month breakdown of what to expect when you visit Orlando. We also give you tricks to avoid long waits for rides, money-saving tips, and recommendations for making your vacation a magical one!

LEAST-CROWDED MONTHS

1. **September**
   Summer weather continues throughout September in Central Florida. Expect far fewer crowds than in the summer months of June, July, and August. Halloween decorations will spread throughout Universal Studios Florida most of the month. The popular Halloween Horror Nights also begins in the middle of September. While the weekends for this event will be packed, the weekdays have the thinnest crowds.

2. **February**
   The Resort typically has fewer crowds at this time, though weekends can be fairly busy. Still, we find that February is one of the better months for cooler weather, sparse crowds, and less expensive hotel rates.

3. **January**
   After the holidays and when children return back to school, the crowd levels at the Universal Orlando Resort suddenly drop. Though some holiday weekend around Presidents' Day and MLK Jr. Day could be busier, it's generally a quieter month.

MOST-CROWDED MONTHS

1. **July**
   Massive crowds from all over the world flood Orlando. Expect long lines, and some of the hottest, most humid weather of the year.

2. **December**
   While park guests are treated to holiday decor and special attractions, the crowds are some of the most massive. If you must go in December, the first week is often the least crowded.

3. **August**
   Similar to July with the crowds, but August doesn't get as busy until after the first week. Keep in mind that the weather is blazing hot in Central Florida in August.

> **Note:** Are you planning to be at the Resort during one of the busier months? Don't worry! This guide will help you avoid those long lines. Be sure to follow one of our pre-planned attraction lists at the end of the book – we use them ourselves, and they can save you hours of time waiting in lines (or help you avoid them altogether).

DAY BREAKDOWN

Sunday
Weekend crowds, but far less than Saturday.

Monday
Often Mondays can be just as crowded as Sundays because guests take off extra days to avoid weekend traffic. Mondays directly after a holiday can also be very packed.

Tuesday
Typically the fewest crowds and the shortest lines.

Wednesday
The second-best day for fewer crowds and shorter lines.

Thursday
Third-best day for fewer crowds, but still busier than most Tuesdays and Wednesdays.

Friday
Less busy in the morning, but busiest in the evening after school when the locals tend to visit. CityWalk can be open later but gets swamped with Floridians experiencing the nightlife.

Saturday
By far, the busiest day at the Resort.

BEST DAYS TO VISIT

These days always depend on the month, but this is a general idea of how to avoid the largest crowds.

1. The first or second weeks in February (especially Tuesdays and Wednesdays)
2. The last week in January (unless it's near the Martin Luther King, Jr. Day Holiday on the third Monday of January)
3. Second week of September (but not around Labor Day)

MORE DATES TO CONSIDER

Weekdays – Like we said before, weekdays are the best times to plan your trip!

Holidays – Due to national holidays, these are the most visited times. Here is the list of the most popular holidays:

- Christmas (all week)
- New Year's (all week)
- Thanksgiving (all week)
- Easter (all week)
- The 4th of July (all week)

- Memorial Day weekend
- Labor Day weekend
- Martin Luther King Jr. weekend
- Presidents' Day week
- Columbus Day
- Veteran's Day weekend
- Mother's Day
- Father's Day

MORE TIPS

Universal's tier pricing will be higher ("Anytime" pricing) on more crowded days and lower ("Value" pricing) on less crowded days. You can view a calendar on Universal's website, **www.UniversalOrlando.com**, to see how busy they anticipate your visit to be.

MONTH BREAKDOWN

JANUARY

Overview: January is busy in the first two weeks, and generally less busy after that. The first week will be crowded and filled with holiday attractions and decorations lighting the Resort.

Weather: Mid-70°F (mid-20°C) during the day and chilly at night (sometimes in the 40s° F / 4-9° C). The humidity is low.

Least Crowded Days: The last week in January.

Most Crowded Days: The first two weeks (especially around New Year's) and Martin Luther King Jr. Weekend (Friday through Monday).

New Year's EVE Celebration:

CityWalk hosts a massive annual event on December 31st called EVE. Live DJs, decorations, and food all come with the

event that lasts from 8pm until 2am. This is a separate ticketed one-night event.
Tickets: UniversalOrlando.com

FEBRUARY

Overview: Typically, the least crowded month to visit the Universal Orlando Resort.
Weather: Mid-70°F (mid-20°C) during the day and chilly at night (low 50s° F / 10-12°C). Also expect far less humidity than in the summer and fall. The humidity is low.
Least Crowded Days: Any week except near Presidents' Day week.
Most Crowded Days: President's Day week
Mardi Gras: All month, Universal Studios hosts a Mardi Gras celebration with delicious New Orleans food, music events, and stilt walkers. This is a popular event that comes with your ticket.

SPECIAL EVENT: MARDI GRAS

Mid-February through March or Early April
See live music concerts and sample New Orleans cuisine in this lively festival. There's also a nighttime Mardi Gras parade with plenty of beads and family-friendly floats. We recommend watching the parade on the corner of Hollywood Blvd near the park entrance for the best experience (and the most beads)! You may be able to access a virtual line pass via the Universal Orlando app to allow reserved access to the parade.

MARCH

Overview: March's popularity has increased recently as spring breaks spread throughout the month. If you visit in March, be sure to do so during the week, Tuesday through Thursday.

Weather: mid-70°F (21°C) during the day and chilly at night. However, March has been known to have occasional heatwaves, bringing the weather above 90°F (32°C).
Least Crowded Days: the first Tuesday, Wednesday, and Thursday of March.
Most Crowded: Last two weeks of the month for Spring Break.
Mardi Gras: The event continues through March at Universal Studios.

APRIL

Overview: With Spring Breaks continuing through April, the end of the month tends to be the least crowded. We love visiting in April because the weather feels warm, but a lot less humid than the summer and fall months.
Weather: Low-80°F (25-28°C) during the day and cooler at night (mid-60°F / 15-19°C). The humidity is medium.
Least Crowded Days: The last two weeks of the month.
Most Crowded Days: The weeks before and after Easter.

MAY

Overview: Spring in Orlando is beautiful, but very warm. To most, it will feel like the Floridian summer has begun. Storms tend to pick up during this time and it might rain during the day for an hour or so. However, the rain is warm and the rides are set up for the short showers, so it shouldn't put a damper on your vacation.

Weather: Mid-70°F (21°C) during the day and sometimes chilly at night. The humidity is medium/high.
Least Crowded Days: The first two weeks of the month.
Most Crowded Days: Memorial Day weekend (Friday through Tuesday).

DEAL: SUMMER TICKET OFFER

Universal Orlando often rolls out a summer ticket package where guests receive additional free ticket days. For example, the deal may offer 5-day tickets for the price of 2 days! You can usually find these deals posted on UniversalOrlando.com.

JUNE

Overview: Mild summer weather perfect for water rides and pool time fun!

Weather: Mid-80°F (27°C) during the day. Typically keeps warm at night. The humidity is medium/high.

Least Crowded Days: Tuesdays, Wednesdays, and Thursdays and the first week of the month.

Most Crowded Days: The last week of the month.

JULY

Overview: The weather heats up—often, unbearably so—and crowds from all over the world pour into the Universal Orlando Resort. Even though July is crowded, it does make a great opportunity to visit Volcano Bay and ride the many water-based attractions at the theme parks.

Weather: Low-90°F during the day, but the humidity can make July feel even warmer. The weather typically stays warm and humid at night. The humidity is high.

Least Crowded Days: Tuesdays, Wednesdays, and Thursdays (unless one is July 4th)

Most Crowded Days: July 4th

Fourth of July: See a fireworks spectacular at Universal Studios Florida throughout the night. This is the same fireworks display, but done with a bit more flare.

Note: As we've said before, July is the busiest month. If you are planning to visit during this time, see our tips for beating the crowds at the end of this chapter.

AUGUST

Overview: Just when you think Florida couldn't get any hotter than in July, August comes around. August is typically the hottest month. The weather continues to heat up even more and crowds continue to pour in until school begins around mid-August. However, August rarely feels as crowded as July.
Weather: Mid-90°F (32°C) during the day with usually near 100% humidity. Nights are sometimes just as warm and balmy. Showers typically occur once a day for an hour or two, but the queues for most rides have coverings. The humidity is very high.
Least Crowded Days: Tuesdays, Wednesdays, and Thursdays, and the last two weeks of the month.
Most Crowded Days: The first two weeks of the month.

· Magic Tips ·
Don't forget the water! Bring your own water bottle to save money. You can refill your bottle at various locations around the park including drinking fountains.

SEPTEMBER

Overview: More hot weather typically all month long with Halloween Horror Nights beginning in the middle of the month (see October for details).
Weather: High-90°F (32°C) during the day. Typically keeps very warm at night. The humidity is very high.
Least Crowded Days: Tuesdays, Wednesdays, Thursdays, and Fridays.
Most Crowded Days: Labor Day weekend.

OCTOBER

Overview: As the weather cools, the monsters come out to play! See the scary side of Universal Orlando at the special event, Halloween Horror Nights. A warning: gory decorations may be left up during the daytime.

Weather: High-80°F (29-31°C) during the day, cools a bit at night. The later you go in October, the more likely tropical storms can come into play. If you are planning a visit, we recommend somewhere in the first couple of weeks. The humidity is very high.

Least Crowded Days: Tuesdays, Wednesdays, and Thursdays.

Most Crowded Days: Evenings when guests visit before Halloween Horror Nights.

SPECIAL EVENT: HALLOWEEN HORROR NIGHTS

A special event for after dark, when the parks close. See monster movies and horror television come to life in intricate mazes, terrifying displays, and vengeful murderers running the streets. Every year the themes change, so you'll never know what to expect! Later on, we cover Halloween Horror Nights in more detail.

NOVEMBER

Overview: The holidays begin mid-November at the Universal Orlando Resort. Expect larger crowds beginning Veterans Day and onward (see December for holiday details).

Weather: High-70°F during the day, cools at night to High-50°F. The humidity is medium.

Least Crowded Days: The first week of the month.

Most Crowded: Veteran's Day weekend and Thanksgiving week.

SPECIAL EVENT: THANKSGIVING

Thursday, November 28, 2024

If you are planning your stay during the holiday, make your reservation for one of these hotel dining experiences (subject to change):

Aventura Hotel – The Urban Pantry hosts a Thanksgiving feast with traditional favorites.

Cabana Bay Beach – The Bayline Diner offers a traditional Thanksgiving lunch and dinner with turkey, mashed potatoes, stuffing, gravy, and yams for guests.

Sapphire Falls – Amatista Cookhouse offers a Thanksgiving breakfast and dinner buffet with characters (dinner only).

Royal Pacific Resort – Jake's American Bar serves breakfast and the Islands Dining Room serves a lunch and dinner character buffet with traditional Thanksgiving favorites.

Hard Rock Hotel – The Avalon Ballroom hosts a Thanksgiving Day breakfast buffet. The Kitchen Restaurant serves a Thanksgiving buffet for lunch and dinner. Expect traditional favorites as well as seafood. Characters, a magician, and other entertainment show up for this event.

Portofino Bay – Trattoria del Porto and Mama Della's Ristorante serve a lunch and dinner buffet with traditional Thanksgiving dining. Both offer entertainment like live music.

UNIVERSAL'S HOLIDAY EXPERIENCE featuring Macy's Balloons

See special characters on Christmastime floats at the Universal Studios Florida theme park! Many of the floats are from the Macy's Day Parade and look amazing as they stroll through the park. This event runs around Thanksgiving through the first week of January.

· **Magic Tips** ·

The holiday parade route runs from Hollywood through New York. We recommend standing near the Revenge of the Mummy ride in New York for the easiest viewing. Either side of the street should have more space and a clear view for photos.

DECEMBER

Overview: The holidays roll in with a *Harry Potter*-themed Christmas celebration. Not all is merry, however, as the Grinch stomps into Seuss Landing.
Weather: Low-70°F (21-23 °C) during the day, cools at night to Low-50°F (10-12°C). The humidity is low.
Least Crowded Days: The first week of the month.
Most Crowded: The last two weeks, especially Christmas Day and New Year's Eve.
Universal Holiday Parade
The Macy's Day parade floats come south to Universal Studios Florida in this exciting daytime celebration.

THE WIZARDING WORLD CHRISTMAS

Harry Potter fans, rejoice for the magic of Christmas and the Wizarding World come together in a magical way! Hogsmeade and Diagon Alley are well-decorated for this stunning event. Drink hot Butterbeer while you watch the nighttime spectacular at Hogwarts Castle with unforgettable projections and dazzling special effects!

SPECIAL EVENT: CHRISTMAS

Monday, December 25, 2024
The following hotels offer Christmas Day Feasts:
Aventura Hotel – The Urban Pantry
Cabana Bay Beach – The Bayline Diner
Sapphire Falls – Amatista Cookhouse (Christmas breakfast buffet and a Christmas dinner character buffet)
Royal Pacific Resort – Jake's American Bar serves breakfast and the Islands Dining Room serves a lunch and dinner character buffet.

Hard Rock Hotel – The Avalon Ballroom hosts a Christmas Day breakfast buffet and the Kitchen Restaurant serves a Christmas character buffet for lunch and dinner.
Portofino Bay – Trattoria del Porto serves a lunch buffet with traditional Christmas dining. Universal characters, other entertainers, and a craft table spread around the room.

MORE HOLIDAY EVENTS

Hanukkah Menorah Lighting Ceremony – Hosted in each hotel at sundown during Hanukkah.

Santa Claus Visit – Santa stops by the Hard Rock Hotel, Portofino Bay, and Cabana Bay Beach Resort on select nights in December.

Universal's Holiday Viewing Party – For an additional cost during the week of Christmas, get reserved seating for the daytime parade and nighttime water show. In addition, you'll receive holiday desserts and drinks with this add-on option. This works great as a midday break for those wishing to have a closer view with some dessert options during the busy time of year. These tickets are priced around $50 each ($30 for kids 3-9) on top of required theme park admission.

SPECIAL EVENT: NEW YEAR'S EVE

Sunday, December 31, 2024
CityWalk hosts a massive annual event on December 31st called EVE. Live DJs, special effects, and food all come with the event that lasts from 8pm until 2am. Tickets range from about $110 to $200 per adult (21+ only). VIP tickets include drink tickets and access to private bars, food, and a special entrance to avoid the crowds. Universal Annual Passholders save 10% when purchasing in advance. Prices usually increase after December 15th.
Tickets may be purchased at UniversalOrlando.com.

BEAT THE CROWDS

1. **Be Early** – Get to the park at opening before the crowds. If you are staying at a Universal Orlando Resort hotel, you can get early entry to the *Harry Potter* attractions in both parks. Since these are the most popular areas, it can save you quite a bit of time, though the hours can start as early as 7:00am.

2. **Plan Your Day** – Follow one of our pre-set day plans at the end of this guide. We use these planners ourselves, and they will save you hours of time waiting in long lines —or help you skip them altogether!

3. **Avoid Typical Meal Times** – If you don't have a restaurant reservation, these are the times to go busy days:
   Lunch: Dine before 11:30am and after 2:30pm
   Dinner: Dine before 5:00pm and after 7:30pm

4. **Get Express Pass** – These premium passes skip the bulk of the line to most attractions at Universal Orlando. However, Express Pass does come with a steep cost (about an additional $100 for both parks). Express Pass Unlimited comes at no extra charge with your stay at the Hard Rock Hotel, Portofino Bay Hotel, or Royal Pacific Hotel. There is a separate fee for Express Pass to Volcano Bay, even if you're staying on property.

· **Magic Tips** ·
During very busy dates, the Universal Orlando theme parks can hit capacity. This typically only affects guests who have not purchased a ticket before their visit and/or are not staying at a Universal Orlando Resort hotel. For this reason, we recommend visiting the parks early—especially during the holidays.

WHAT TO BRING

1. **What to Wear** – Shorts, t-shirts, sneakers (trainers), and tank tops are seen all around the Resort for a good reason: they are comfortable. You'll be standing in the hot (and often humid) Florida sun all day, so we recommend that you dress comfortably. Even on a hot day Orlando can get chilly at night. We highly recommend taking a jacket or sweater to keep you warm during the winter.

2. **Hats, Sunglasses, and Sunscreen** – Again, the Floridian sun! It's a wonderful thing, but you don't want to get burned. Be careful of hats and sunglasses on rides (most high-speed attractions will have a compartment on the ride or a locker to store your belongings).

3. **Stroller** – You can bring your own or rent one at one of the parks. If you're even worried a little that your child may be too tired to walk around all day, it's best to use caution and set aside extra cash for a stroller rental.

4. **Water Bottles and Snacks** – You can save money (or help any picky eaters in your party) by bringing your own snacks. Universal will allow you to bring sealed bottles of water into the parks. If you don't mind fountain water, you can refill at water fountains near any restroom for free.

5. **Hand Sanitizer** – Though we know that science tells us not to use hand sanitizer on a daily basis, it's virtually a must-have at the theme parks. Sometimes you've gone to the restroom a half hour before eating, and the lines are long to wash your hands. You'll likely touch handrails, seat cushions, and many other things that will require you to disinfect before touching food.

6. **Extra Phone Charger** – If you have a smartphone, we highly recommend an extra portable charger. We also

recommend becoming familiar enough with your smartphone so that you can switch on the battery-saver mode in the settings. This will prevent you from running out of juice too early while you take pictures and use the Universal Studios app.

7. **Waterproof Bag** – If you plan on riding the water attractions—like Jurassic Park River Adventure—you're likely to get wet. The last thing you want is to accidentally drench your cellphone! If your device isn't water resistant, bring a plastic sandwich bag for each phone to keep them dry (this also works great for wallets).

8. **A Standard Backpack** – Carry your items in one of these. Make sure it's not too large to fit on the rides. Also keep in mind that your bag will be checked by security before entering the park area. If you don't feel like lugging it around all day, rent a locker after the entrance to each park and store it in there. Pricing starts at $12 per day depending on the size of locker you choose.

· **Magic Tips** ·

Universal may require you to store bags, purses, and other loose items such as sunglasses in single-use lockers while you ride. These free lockers are just to be used while riding and are located near the attraction. Typically, a Universal Team Member will direct you where to store your things. However, these lockers are small—14" x 5.5" x 16.9" (about 35.5 cm x 14cm x 43cm). Since most bags won't fit in that size, larger lockers are available starting at $2 for your ride. We recommend being mindful of the size bag you bring, or rent an all-day locker to save some money.

9. **Money** – The Universal Orlando Resort accepts all major credit cards and cash. However, if you are staying at a Resort hotel, you can link your hotel key card to your credit card for easy paying. Volcano Bay visitors can link a

credit card to their TapuTapu bracelet via the Universal Orlando application. This way you can eat and not worry about soaking your credit card or visiting a locker.

10. **Identification** – For adults, make sure you plan on bringing your government-issued ID if you plan to drink alcoholic beverages. At times, you may be asked to present ID when purchasing at shops in CityWalk.

11. **Water Resistant Clothing** – Even on the sunniest days, rainclouds can show up at the Resort. Typically, the rain will last under two hours, but you don't want to wear something that can't get wet. Leave the suede shoes at home and stick to quick-drying cotton shirts. Just in case you don't want to deal with the rain, this is what we recommend bringing with you:
    Compact Umbrella – On rainy days, this is very handy. Don't bring a full-sized umbrella, as it won't fit on rides and will be difficult to carry around.
    Poncho – It might be a bit of a fashion *faux pas* to some, but a poncho could keep you and your belongings dry. Many visitors love wearing these for the water rides as well!

UNIVERSAL ORLANDO APP

Universal Orlando has developed a free mobile application for accessing important information around the parks. See ride wait times for popular attractions, a map of the theme parks, park hours, and even access a "virtual line" for select rides and attractions.

You can also set up payment methods through the mobile app. This allows you to create spending limits for your family members as well as view receipts. Simply add in your card information and select from the menu list to create your settings.

Once you've synced your card, you can also create mobile food orders for select dining locations. This feature allows for quick and easy ordering without the hassle of waiting in long lines. We list dining options for mobile ordering in the Dining chapter of this guide.

· Magic Tips ·

You can make contactless payments with Universal Pay on the Universal Orlando app. Find the "My Wallet" button and you'll be able to save your credit card. To make a contactless payment, present your QR code in "My Wallet" for the Team Member to scan.

VIRTUAL LINE EXPERIENCE

Several popular attractions use a free Virtual Line Experience to access the queue. Universal uses this pass so that guests spend less time waiting in lines. The Virtual Line Experience can be accessed once you're inside of the theme parks. To use it, log into the Universal Orlando app and click the attraction you wish to experience, and find the button for the Virtual Line Pass. From there, you'll be able to select a return time for your party. The app will then issue your party a QR code. Once your time slot becomes available, head to the attraction queue, show your QR code to the Universal Team Member, and enter the shorter line.

· Magic Tips ·

Universal often allows guests to line up 5 minutes before their Virtual Line time. If you're running late, they may also give you a few minutes of cushion. We also recommend taking a screenshot of your QR code just in case you have trouble pulling it up later. That way, you can easily access the code from your photos instead of reloading the app.

Depending on availability, you may be able to book several virtual spots for the same attraction. Typically, the Universal mobile app works no matter which theme park you visit. Meaning, you may be able to access the Virtual Queue for Hagrid's Motorbike Adventure while in Universal Studios Florida.

Some attractions use both a virtual and a standard queue. For example, some rides like *Fast & Furious – Supercharged* will use a Virtual Line at the start of the day and then later switch to a standard queue. Really, it depends on how busy the parks are and how much demand there is for a ride. Use the Universal Mobile app to check which method your desired attraction is using.

UNIVERSAL PHOTOS

Universal Orlando offers a photo package for downloads of your theme park pictures. These snapshots are taken by Universal photographers around the parks. It's a great way to capture the best moments and have some great images to share online. The photographers are also trained to help you pose in amazing ways that capture the scene—Hollywood magic!

Prices start at $69.99 for one day and $89.99 for three days (plus tax). There are usually around a dozen or so photo spots in each park. Our favorites are the Harry Potter and the Escape from Gringotts In-Queue Photo Op (Diagon Alley, Universal Studios Florida) and the Raptor Encounter Photo Op (Jurassic Park, Islands of Adventure). However, Volcano Bay also has some fun photo op spots! If you just want photos for Volcano Bay, a 1-day pass is just $39.99 (plus tax). Visit UniversalOrlando.com to purchase your photo package. You'll also need the Amazing Pictures Mobile App to download your photos.

· Magic Tips ·
Share your Universal photos with the hashtag #UniversalMoments and you could get featured on their social media!

HEALTH & SAFETY

In March of 2020, the Universal Orlando Resort closed its gates to all guests due to the COVID-19 pandemic. The Resort reopened a few months later in June to sparse crowds. At the time, many health and safety restrictions were enforced —including physical distancing guidelines and required face coverings. However, by summer of 2021, most of these restrictions lifted at the Resort.

In the event that increased health and safety guidelines return and the parks remain open, Universal Orlando could bring back some of these former measures. Previously, visiting guests were required to wear face coverings and maintain physical distance from other parties. In addition, not all dining spots, attractions, and experiences were available. Universal Team Members were also expected to abide by the same rules by wearing face coverings and maintaining safe distances from guests.

Of course, we're only covering this to help set your expectations should such an event reoccur. Universal could change its requirements for health and safety reasons as more information becomes available. If the pandemic severity level changes, we may also see an update in some mandatory regulations.

Note: It's important to understand that the entire world is coming to grips with a global pandemic. While we do our best to give you fresh tips for your visit, some of these social distancing measures may change. It's also important that you visit UniversalOrlando.com and read their protocols for social distancing, safety, and guest health.

Additionally, you will want to ensure that your state, county, or country won't be impacted by your trip. Some places may have travel restrictions for Florida and vice versa.

CHAPTER TWO

BOOKING YOUR TRIP

TIPS BEFORE YOUR BOOK

For all vacation planning, we always recommend booking as far in advance as possible. However, Universal often has last-minute hotel rooms that could still save you a bundle. The only exceptions are the Hard Rock and Portofino Bay hotels which tend to book up quickly. Last-minute cancellations occur and you can still get a great discount, especially during the less busy times. If you're traveling by air, we recommend Orlando International because it tends to be the least expensive and easiest to travel from. The airport is located right next to highways that will take you to Universal, which is only about 20 minutes away by car.

If you are planning to exclusively stay at the Universal Orlando Resort, you likely won't need a rental car. Simply call a cab, ride share service, or use your hotel's transport to get from the airport to the Resort. Many hotels outside of the Resort will also provide free transport to the parks. Even if you are planning a day at Disney, but staying at Universal, we recommend saving money and skipping the rental car. Not only will the car cost you, but so will parking at the Resort. We'll review parking costs and all transport options next.

TICKET TYPES

Park Ticket

Single-Day park tickets vary in pricing for each day, depending on the predicted crowd size. In other words, normal weekdays are less expensive than weekends and holidays. Universal has many options and add-on features that can be a bit difficult to understand on their website, so we've simplified it here:

Advanced Ticket Prices – Adult and Child

Child tickets are for ages 3-9. Adult tickets are for all guests age 10 or older. Children under 3 get in free.

Adult Tickets – Starting at $109 for most weekdays and off-season dates. Prices go as high as $159 per park.

Child Tickets (Ages 3-9) – Starting at $104 for most weekdays and off-season dates. Prices go as high as $154 per park.

Volcano Bay – Starting at $80 for adults and $75 for children 3-9, per day.

Park-to-Park Tickets – Starting at $164 for adults and $159 for children ages 3-9. Visit either park as many times as you'd like in one day.

Multi-Day Tickets

Save when you purchase multiple-date tickets for your visit. The best deals start at three days or more.

Annual Passes

Universal offers several annual passes starting at $304.99 for a seasonal pass that works at both Universal Studios Florida and Universal's Islands of Adventure. Some of these annual passes have blockout dates. However, if you're visiting during a less-busy time for multiple dates, an annual pass could save you money. Annual Passes also come with several perks including free or discounted parking, event tickets, early park admission, and hotel discounts.

Parking Cost for Theme Parks

- $27 for standard self-parking
- $40-$60 for closer Prime Parking (price varies by date)
- $32 for RV/Bus
- Valet is also available for 2-hour windows starting at $27 (varies by date)

> **· Magic Tips ·**
> After 6pm, self-parking is free (not valid during Halloween Horror Nights).
>
> Parking is free with 2 paid matinee tickets (11am - 6pm) to the Universal Cinemark movie theatre. Parking must be prepaid and will be reimbursed after purchasing tickets.

Bundle

Sometimes purchasing a flight/hotel/car package from **www.UniversalOrlando.com** or a third party travel website can save you a lot of money. If you collect points with airlines like Southwest or Alaska, you can get even better bonuses with a bundle.

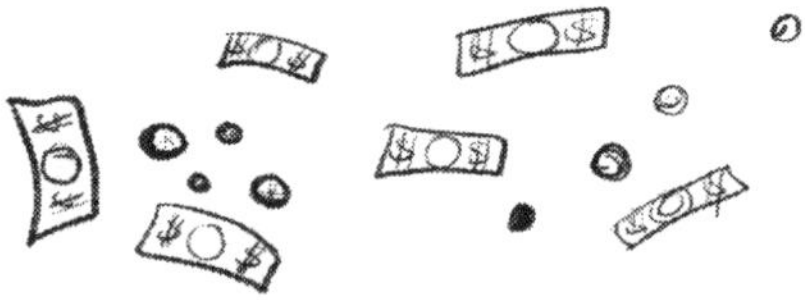

EXPRESS PASS TIPS

Express Pass is a paid feature that works in conjunction with an admission ticket. This unique pass allows guests to "cut the line" to nearly every attraction in Universal Studios Florida and Universal's Islands of Adventure. Express Pass allows for skipping the main line once per ride per day while Express Pass *Unlimited* allows for as many skips as they'd like. Guests can even ride an attraction over and over again, back to back!

Express Pass Unlimited starts at about $20 more than the standard Express Pass. Guests can also select Express Pass at just one park or both. The busiest days may also charge more or run out of Express Passes, so we always recommend purchasing in advance.

TIPS FOR BUYING EXPRESS PASS

1. **Get One Free** – Guests staying at the Hard Rock Hotel, Portofino Bay, or Royal Pacific Hotels get free Express Pass Unlimited as part of their reservation. Hotel Express Passes also work all day on your date of checkout.
2. **Book Ahead** – Universal only distributes so many Express Passes each day, so we recommend booking in advance. Express Passes are usually cheaper when booked ahead and may sell out before your visit.
3. **You Can Still Buy There** – If you change your mind last minute and decide to purchase an Express Pass, see an Express Pass distributor inside of the park and upgrade your ticket (if Express Pass is still available). Look for the "Express Pass Sold Here" sign at vendors in the parks.
4. **Late Arrival** – On less-busy days, Universal may offer a discounted Express Pass that works after 4pm. If available, these passes can be purchased during the day at Express Pass distribution locations in the parks.

· Magic Tips ·

Please note that hotel Express Pass works for the two theme parks and not the Volcano Bay water park.

Notes

1. Not all Park-to-Park tickets include Volcano Bay. Only the 3-Park tickets include all three of the Resort parks. You may add on Volcano Bay to your multi-day ticket at a discounted bundled price.
2. Tickets have date limitations, so be careful not to purchase too far in advance. We have seen people turned away from the gates for expired and incorrect tickets.
3. Prices may increase or decrease throughout the year.
4. Express Passes are an add-on to your Universal Studios or Island of Adventure ticket and they can be purchased together or separately, but you must have a park ticket to use Express Pass and Express Pass Unlimited.
5. Florida residents can save even more on tickets, up to $80 off ticket promotions, but you must have a valid Florida ID to get this discount. Blockout days may apply for these specially prices tickets. For more information about Florida resident discounts, visit **UniversalOrlando.com.**

· **Magic Tips** ·

Volcano Bay also offers Express Pass options. We cover those later in the chapter for this water park. Keep in mind that hotel Express Passes only work at the two main theme parks.

VIP EXPERIENCE

Starting at $189/person on top of the standard day ticket

Universal Orlando offers a fantastic ticket upgrade with a VIP Experience. Just book a one- or two-park ticket and select the VIP add-on feature instead of an Express Pass. This experience has access to behind-the-scenes looks in a guided tour. As a VIP, you'll be able to cut the line to most attractions, including the ones in the Wizarding World.

We recommend VIP if you're heavily interested in backstage exclusives and how Universal Orlando operates. The tour also comes with several perks including a complimentary lunch, cut-the-line privileges for at least 10 rides, reserved show seating, valet parking, and even discounts at select merchandise locations. After the tour (which lasts 4-5 hours), you'll receive an Express Pass for the rest of the day. Keep in mind that VIP Experiences may lump your group with others unless you book a private tour at an increased cost.

· Magic Tips ·
Universal Orlando may also offer a VIP Holiday Tour with many of the same benefits. In the past, Universal has offered these tours exclusive access to Grinchmas, Universal's Holiday Experience featuring Macy's Balloons, and a special showing of The Magic of Christmas at Hogwarts Castle.

BOOKING WITH DISCOUNTS

There are many ways to save on booking a stay at Universal Orlando. Some offers are better than others depending on the deal. Here are our most recommended booking sites based on total savings. When visiting, we often book with Orbitz for their extra discount on the hotel and then book the tickets separately through **www.UniversalOrlando.com**.

AMERICAN EXPRESS

American Express is the official credit card for the Universal Orlando Resort, which means you can use it for special perks and discounts.

1. American Express Lounge – Take a break in this exclusive lounge only for American Express cardholders. The lounge is located in Universal Studios Florida (not Islands of Adventure) and provides free snacks, waters, and a concierge. The lounge is located in New York City and open from 12pm – 5pm.
2. Reserved Seating – Get special reserved seating in the American Express Reserved Parade Viewing area at Universal Studios. Present your American Express card at

the viewing area across from the Brown Derby Hat Shop in Hollywood. You must get there at least 15 minutes before the parade time. Seating is first come, first served.

3. Discounted Dining Plan – Use your American Express card to purchase a Quick Service Universal Dining Plan and receive 10% off.

Note: These offers may expire at any time.

UNIVERSALORLANDO.COM – *Best for Tickets*

1. Check the website for discounts on hotels and more. Here you can book any of the Resort hotels, purchase theme park tickets, and add features like Express Pass.
2. Summer Time (June through August) and Fall (September through October) typically have the lowest fares. However, Universal will offer discounts even for Spring and Winter getaways. Look for deals when booking on the website.

· Magic Tips ·

Universal Orlando has a price match guarantee for its tickets. If you find proof of a better deal, you may be eligible for a price match and a $25 credit for your vacation! To claim this deal, contact Universal at 407-817-8215.

Military Discounts

Universal offers ticket and hotel packages for those who have served and are currently serving in the United States military. For more information and to see current deals, visit their website: **https://site.universalorlando.com/military/**

Other Sites

There are almost countless other options for finding discounts in Orlando. The best deals are typically when you bundle a flight, hotel, and park tickets as one package. Those with AAA memberships, Amex Travel offers, and other affiliations could save a bit more booking through those vendors. We recommend comparing a few third-party sites to ensure you are truly getting the best discount available for your accommodations.

INTRODUCTION

With the planning out of the way, it's time to bring your vacation to the Universal Orlando Resort. Getting there doesn't have to be tricky, but if you don't plan correctly, it could feel very stressful. Most visitors fly into Orlando International Airport when they travel by air. If you have a family of three or more and live within a comfortable driving distance, then traveling by car might be your cheapest option. However, driving may be out of the question if you live on the West Coast, in the Midwest—or further. Thankfully, there are many options to visit Universal Orlando. In fact, you can arrive at the Resort via bus, train, shuttle, or rideshare like Uber or Lyft!

In this chapter, we review the several different methods of getting to the Resort. How you get there is entirely up to you, but if you're feeling indecisive (or just need more information in order to choose), read thoroughly to review the best choices.

BY AIRLINE

If you aren't planning a road trip and live far away from the Resort, flying will likely be your quickest method. While airlines can be expensive at times, there are several ways to save money:

1. Compare airlines to see the best pricing.
2. Check baggage fees and allowed carry-on items. If you live on the East Coast, Spirit Airlines is an *à la carte* option that can save you hundreds of dollars, especially on last-minute flights.
3. Book early, if you can, to get the best discounts.

FLIGHTS WITHIN THE U.S.A.

Southwest

We love Southwest. If you grab their "Wanna Get Away" deals, you can score some great rates. Southwest works perfectly if you book ahead. However, if you are late to the game, they can get pretty pricey. We love Southwest because the staff is friendly, the aircrafts are generally comfortable for long flights, they include complimentary snacks and soft drinks, and you get two free checked luggage bags per person. Free bags are very hard to find these days in the United States, so this is a great deal!

Southwest doesn't charge for change fees, meaning, if you have to change your flight for whatever reason, you can do so without charge during an allotted time period (but you can't receive a refund). Because Southwest offers first-come-first-served seating, we highly recommend paying the extra money to get the "Early Bird" option. This will allow everyone in your party to pick seats together for your flight. Before boarding, you can ask their helpful staff members to assist with seating your family together, though it can't be guaranteed.

Alaska

We also love Alaska Airlines for its updated aircrafts and well-rounded service. Book early enough, and their rates are very affordable. Alaska gives you the free option to select your seat, but checked bags are often at a moderately priced additional charge. Alaska also offers free soft drinks and snacks for their flights. From the West Coast, Alaska is usually one of the few airlines that offers nonstop flights. If you've never flown Alaska, we invite you to give them a try!

Delta

Delta is a premium airline that excels in what it does. While it's not as innovative with its deals as Southwest, it does deliver fantastic flights and aircrafts. This is usually our third choice above other airlines like United or American because of Delta's quality. Those traveling from the East Coast may be able to find fantastic deals when flying Delta to Orlando. However, for West Coasters, Delta is often much more expensive than Southwest or Alaska.

Spirit Airlines – *Budget Option*

This airline is an *à la carte* airline, so the first price you see is just for a seat on the plane—everything else is an extra cost. The extra costs include: picking your own seat, checking a bag or putting a bag in the overhead compartment, drinks, and snacks. If you don't mind where you sit and only need to bring a personal item, Spirit can save you some big bucks. However, once you pick a seat and opt to bring another bag (even carry-on bags are extra), the prices begin to stack. Also, Spirit Airlines doesn't have much of a customer service department in our opinion. We've had an issue with a delayed flight and no one was there to assist at the gate. However, we've had a good experience with them as well. Just understand that you usually get what you pay for and Spirit is no exception to that rule.

Frontier Airlines – *Budget Option*

Works similarly to Spirit and can get to be very pricey. We find that Spirit tends to have more comfortable seats than Frontier. If you're only on a two-hour flight or less, you may not mind. However, Frontier is fine for last-minute flights if you're looking to save and don't need any extra pizazz. Just remember the checked bags are additional.

FROM THE UNITED KINGDOM

KLM-Royal Dutch Airlines
A standard budget airline with plenty of flights from the UK to Orlando International Airport. We've flown KLM before and found that they exceeded our expectations for the price point. You'll have a comfortable seat, efficient boarding, and quality service.

Icelandair
Another competitively priced flying option from Europe. We like Icelandair because not only do they usually have quick flights from the UK, but they also have quality service. We avoid long layovers whenever possible, which Icelandair rarely schedules.

BY CAR

Whether you're on a road trip, staying in a neighboring city, or you live close enough to drive to the Resort, driving can be a great method. On the drive you'll see the beautiful sights of Florida's wetlands before arriving at Universal Orlando.

Car Rental: We recommend Enterprise.com or Dollar.com for car rentals as they typically have a great selection and the best pricing. Pre-booking before you arrive at the airport is advised.

· **Magic Tips** ·
If you are staying on property at the Universal Orlando Resort, we don't recommend a rental car. Parking can cost $30 daily (or more) at the hotels and there are free transports around the Resort. If, however, you plan on visiting Walt Disney World or any other parts of Florida, the car may be worth the fee.

POPULAR RENTAL CAR COMPANIES

- www.Avis.com: Click the "offers" tab for deals. During certain promotional periods, guests who rent Avis cars may receive complimentary parking at Universal Orlando.
- www.Enterprise.com: You can visit the company's website or see typically better deals on Priceline.com (or bundle with your airfare and hotel booking).
- www.Dollar.com: Click the "specials" tab for deals.
- www.Budget.com: Click the "deals" tab for offers.

BY SHUTTLE OR TAXI

Hail a taxi in front of the airport and ask for a flat rate. Rates are usually around $45 each way but can vary depending on demand.

MEARS

For shuttle service from the airport, we recommend Mears. This service usually costs about $23 each way, per person. You can also pay up front for the round trip cost of $37 and they will pick you up from your hotel and return you to the airport at the end of your vacation.

Website: mearstransportation.com (They also have an app).

Note: It is customary to tip your taxi driver 15–20%, depending on your experience with the route.

BY TRAIN

Taking the train can be a relaxing and beautiful way to travel to Universal Orlando. The trains let out at the Orlando Station (or Kissimmee) and you will need to have a second transport from the train station to the Resort (which is roughly 20 minutes away by car).

AMTRAK

Perfect for traveling long distances between cities.

Website: Amtrak.com
Check the "Deals" tab for discounts.

BY BUS

There are a few great reasons to take the bus to Universal Orlando:

1. **Saves Money** – This is usually the top reason you might want to go with the bus. Airfare and the train can cost ten times the amount.
2. **It's Relaxing** – The bus can be a calming, easy way to travel from your home to the Resort.
3. **A Discount** – Seniors and students can receive discounted rates on Greyhound.
4. **Greyhound** – Our top pick for bussing services. They have a great reputation and are often the fastest way with the most options to get to Orlando. Keep in mind that the Orlando Bus Station is not near Orlando International or Universal. You'll need to take a private car into the Resort or to your hotel—and that might cost you a lot of money.

BY PRIVATE CAR APP

With ride-sharing apps like Uber or Lyft taking off across the country, it may seem like a top choice for most travelers. These offer private drivers in clean cars (that are not cabs).

Here are a few ways you can book:
Uber or Lyft (mobile application):
To download one of these applications, open the App Store (Apple Devices) or GooglePlay Store (Android Devices) and search for "Lyft" or "Uber" in the store.

- Lyft's least-expensive car option, which seats 4, goes for around $15-$30 each way (depending on traffic).
- You can request a larger car, Lyft XL, which can seat up to 6 for an additional fee which varies by distance.
- When you are ready for your car to arrive, activate it on the app. The pickup spot is in the Express Pick-Up tunnel

located on Level 2 (subject to change). The application should signal where to go. Your driver also will alert you when he/she has arrived.

- When returning to the airport, you can summon a car on the app to pick you up at your hotel. This is usually the same cost as traveling there.

· Magic Tips ·
Uber, Lyft, taxis, and other rideshare apps drop off at the Universal Studios parking garage on the roof level. Hotel guests are dropped off in front of their resort.

TRANSPORT INSIDE UNIVERSAL

Water Taxis
Running every 15-30 minutes, these free taxis travel between the parks and CityWalk to Hard Rock Hotel, Loews Portofino Bay, the Royal Pacific, and Sapphire Falls. This is our favorite method to travel. The water taxis have a covering to shield from the weather and the river is fun for scenery—including the occasional turtle swimming beside the boat.

Shuttles
Free busses will shuttle you between all of the hotels and to the parks and CityWalk. The shuttles run about every 15 minutes.

Walk
All Resort hotels have walking paths to the parks, with Hard Rock being the closest at 5 minutes. The rest are about 10-15 minute walks on paths with signs directing you.

CHAPTER FOUR

UNIVERSAL STUDIOS FLORIDA PARK

THEMED AREAS

The original Universal Studios Orlando theme park brings guests into a faux Hollywood studio backlot. Yet, so that the theme doesn't tire, Universal created several different areas to explore. From the streets of New York City to the magical world of *Harry Potter*, Universal Studios Florida sets out to impress with thrills.

Production Central

Just like the movies! You'll be surrounded by large sound stages that house the Transformers: The Ride - 3D. Production Central eventually turns into a small outdoor amphitheater where live concerts are sometimes hosted.

Minion Land

The zany and colorful world of Minions comes to life in this land! Experience family-friendly attractions including *Despicable Me* Minion Mayhem or and Illumination's Villain-Con Minion Blast. There are also Minions-themed dining, shopping, and character meets!

New York
The details of the New York lot are incredible! From pizzerias to the museum facade that hosts the Revenge of the Mummy roller coaster, you'll feel part of a real-life New York movie set!

San Francisco
Like New York, but with a West Coast vibe. San Francisco runs along a studio lagoon and features the high-speed simulator, Fast and the Furious – Supercharged.

World Expo
A swanky, World Expo-themed area with a theatre and the crazy alien shootout ride, Men in Black Alien Attack!

Springfield: Home of the Simpsons
Experience animated fun on The Simpsons Ride! Adults can grab a beer at Moe's Tavern and families can enjoy the best donut ever, The Big Pink, at Lard Lad Donuts.

Woody Woodpecker's Kidzone
This kid-friendly land is currently undergoing reimagining for new experiences and could be renamed in 2024. The E.T. Adventure ride remains open during construction.

Hollywood
Rounding off the backlot theme, Hollywood brings mid-century charm to its surrounding sound stages and facades. This area is a little dated, but fun nonetheless with a stunt show and fireworks over the lagoon.

Diagon Alley – The Wizarding World of Harry Potter
Right out of the *Harry Potter* films comes a stunning London scene. You'll have to find your way inside Diagon Alley's hidden entrance, but once you do, you'll be magically transported into the Wizarding World of Harry Potter!

PRODUCTION CENTRAL & MINION LAND

RIDES

DESPICABLE ME MINION MAYHEM

Description: A motion simulation ride with moving seats that follows characters from the *Despicable Me* animated film series.
Type: Motion Simulation Ride
Perfect for: Kids, Tweens, Family
Height Restriction: 40"
Review: Even if you're not a fan of *Despicable Me*, this zany and hilarious motion simulation ride should be on your list. The ride line gets pretty long throughout the day, so we recommend experiencing this attraction early on to avoid the increasing wait times.

Note: Non-moving seats are available.

ILLUMINATION'S VILLAIN-CON MINION BLAST

Description: Grab a blaster and move through this attraction that has guests blasting targets! You'll come across villains including Belle Bottom and Jean Clawed.
Type: Moving Sidewalk Blaster Attraction
Perfect for: Kids, Tweens, Family
Height Restriction: Under 48' (122 cm) requires supervising Companion
Review: A family-friendly attraction great for those who enjoy video games. It's not a traditional ride but a moving sidewalk with wireless blasters guests aim at targets. Some point-scoring elements may feel confusing, but if you're okay just blasting at a screen, you'll have fun. Hint: aim for the loot boxes.
Universal App: You can sync your experience to the Universal Orlando app to rack up points and digital collectibles. To

access, open the Universal Florida app on your phone, sign in, and find the "Illumination's Villain-Con Minion Blast" Connected Gameplay tab. Open it, and you'll see how to tap your phone to the blaster and sync your points.

Power-Up: Using the app, you can choose between different blasters: Banana Bomb, Fart Bomb, and Pulverizing Pinball. Each has slightly different effects and zany fun. The regular Banana Bomb will do, though! You'll unlock other options the more you play.

HOLLYWOOD RIP RIDE ROCKIT

Description: A high-speed steel roller coaster where you pick the soundtrack.

Perfect for: Thrill Riders

Height Restriction: 51" minimum and 79" maximum

Car: 2 riders per row

Single Rider Available

Review: The Rip Ride Rockit has a very cool feature of selecting your own music for the ride. Pick from around 30 different songs from pop and rock to country and dance before you ride. Then you'll soar over 16 stories in the sky before dropping nearly straight down at up to 65 miles per hour. It's an exciting, high-speed coaster that's fairly smooth and a lot of fun. For bonus enjoyment, ride the coaster at night when its lights start flashing! You can also get a video done—like a music video—of your ride experience afterward!

If you're not a thrill rider, we highly recommend skipping this one.

> **Note:** If you're worried about comfort, a test seat is available outside of the ride queue. This coaster also does not allow loose items, so you must store them in a locker.

SECRET SONG SELECT

The Hollywood Rip Ride Rockit allows you to choose from a list of songs by genre, but you can hack the ride to unlock additional songs. Here's how:

1. Once you've boarded, instead of selecting a song, press and hold the Rockit logo for 10 seconds until a number pad is displayed.
2. Enter one of the codes below to play your choice of bonus tracks!
   Pop: "Vogue" – Madonna (310) / "The Rainbow Connection" – The Muppets (902)
   Rock: "Break On Through" – The Doors (103) / "Crocodile Rock" – Elton John (104) / "Live" – Lenny Kravitz (115) / "Mexicola" – Queens of the Stone Age (116) / "Start Me Up" – The Rolling Stones (122) / "Run to You" – Bryan Adams (308) / "For Whom the Bell Tolls" – Metallica (703)
   R&B/Hip Hop: "I Want You Back" – The Jackson Five (302) / "Lose Yourself" – Eminem (306) / "My Everything" – Barry White (312)!

> **Note:** When you hack a song with a code, you won't be able to get a video of your ride.

TRANSFORMERS: THE RIDE-3D

Description: An explosive, 3D motion simulation ride starring the robots from the *Transformers* film series.
Perfect for: Kids, Tweens, Teens, Adults, Thrill Riders
Height Restriction: 40"
Car: 4 riders per row
Single Rider Available
Review: Join the Autobots and defeat the evil Decepticons. The ride is very similar to The Amazing Adventures of Spider-Man attraction at Islands of Adventure. However, Transformers has more realistic special effects and action sequences. It's hard not to enjoy the high-energy charm of this ride.

SHOWS AND ATTRACTIONS

MUSIC PLAZA STAGE

Description: Outdoor music stages
Perfect for: All ages
Review: Some dynamic entertainers have performed on this stage. Universal changes up the lineup and makes it even better for summer concerts. For lists of performers, check out their website **www.universalorlando.com**

STREET PERFORMERS

Look for various performances at different times around the Production Central backlot.

NEW YORK

RIDES

REVENGE OF THE MUMMY

Description: An Egyptian-themed indoor roller coaster.
Perfect for: Tweens, Teens, Adults, Thrill Riders
Height Restriction: 48"
Car: 4 riders per row

Virtual Line Pass: Yes
Single Rider Available
Review: Face everything from eerie darkness to pyrotechnic effects as you face the wrath of an ancient mummy. This lengthy roller coaster moves through several rooms before reaching 45 miles per hour just before the climax. We won't give away the ending, but The Mummy is full of sweet revenge. Overall, the ride isn't nearly as intense as Hollywood Rip Ride Rockit, so even families can enjoy this one.

> **Note:** If you're worried about comfort, a test seat is available outside of the ride queue. This coaster also does not allow loose items, so you must store them in a locker.

RACE THROUGH NEW YORK STARRING JIMMY FALLON

Description: 3-D motion simulator.
Perfect for: Kids, Tweens, Teens, Adults
Height Restriction: 40"
Car: 10 riders per row
Virtual Line Pass: Yes
Review: Enter a façade of NBC's New York building and race through the city along with Tonight Show host, Jimmy Fallon. Filled with zany action, Race Through New York is a silly 3-D motion simulator designed as an attraction that everyone can enjoy. The queue looks very cool with decor from the Tonight Show. Unfortunately, Race Through New York is fairly lackluster. Why, of all of its franchises, did Universal decide to create a ride around the Tonight Show? Jimmy Fallon's jokes often miss and his odd assembly of characters pale in comparison to other simulators, like hilarious The Simpsons Ride. To further confuse things, guests are assigned a "group color" that is called when it's their turn to ride. Many times, this isn't properly explained in the waiting room, so employees shout at guests who shuffle into the ride wondering if they are in the correct spot. Overall, Race Through New York is a ride you probably won't care to experience twice.

SHOWS AND ATTRACTIONS

THE BLUES BROTHERS SHOW

Description: Listen to R&B jams performed live by the famous duo.
Perfect for: Adults
Length: 15 min
Review: A classic Universal attraction keeps its mark on the streets of New York. The show is very entertaining, even though the stage is small. In a way, you'll feel like you're watching the real-life Blues Brothers performing right before your eyes. Perfect for classic R&B fans, though most guests may only stop for a song or two.

SAN FRANCISCO

RIDES

FAST & FURIOUS – SUPERCHARGED

Description: A 3D high-speed race simulator starring the characters from the *Fast & Furious* franchise.
Perfect for: Kids, Tweens, Teens, Adults, Thrill Riders
Height Restriction: 40" (48" without adult)
Virtual Line Pass: Yes (sometimes)
Review: Board a "party bus" on the way to an exclusive event starring the *Fast & Furious* characters as disaster strikes! While *Fast & Furious* is one of Universal's most popular franchises, the attraction doesn't quite meet up to the hype of the movies. Sure, there are cameos including Vin Diesel, The Rock, and several cool cars from the films. Fast & Furious – Supercharged unfortunately comes off like a quick and cheesy action simulator with too much build up (there are two showrooms before you actually board the ride) and not enough pay off. Nevertheless, it's still a better overall experience than Race Through New York Starring Jimmy Fallon.

SHOWS AND ATTRACTIONS

STREET PERFORMERS

Look for singing and performing groups at various times throughout the day. Check out your map for show times on the day you arrive.

RIDES

MEN IN BLACK ALIEN ATTACK

Description: A laser-guided shooting ride.
Perfect for: Young Kids, Kids, Tweens, Teens
Height Restriction: 42"
Car: 3 riders per row, 6 per vehicle
Single Rider Available

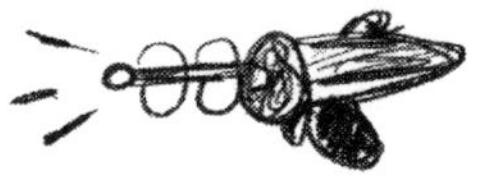

Review: Start your training as an MIB agent by blasting as many aliens as you can with your laser gun. The aliens pop out of everything from street corners to windows as you move along the city. Your score is calculated at the end. The ride is fun for competitive people, but some of the aliens look a bit cheesy. Men in Black feels like a well-done carnival ride and we wish that it was more obvious which aliens were worth more points. However, we've figured it out and have some excellent tips—especially if you like to win!

SCORE THE HIGHEST

Get the highest score by checking out these tips!

1. Hold the Trigger – Keep your finger on the trigger for continuous and rapid firing. Never let go!
2. Small Means Big – The smaller the alien, the bigger the score. Look for hidden aliens popping out of windows and trashcans. They are worth far more than their big brothers.
3. Keep Shooting – Lock on to little targets for as long as you can! You can shoot a target more than once.
4. Time the Bonus – There is a 100,000-point bonus at the end of the ride. Look for the enormous, room-sized bug and listen for Agent Zed to say "Push the Red Button!" Press the button on the dash in front of you and hit it as soon as he says "push." Don't let go of the bonus button and multiple people in your car can get it, too!

SHOWS AND ATTRACTIONS

> **· Magic Tips ·**
> The Fear Factor theater has been closed for quite some time now. Though some speculated the attraction would reopen seasonally, it appears that a new experience will replace the show in the future. However, it's unknown if Universal will add another show here in 2024.

SPRINGFIELD HOME OF THE SIMPSONS

RIDES

THE SIMPSONS RIDE

Description: Motion-simulation ride starring characters from *The Simpsons*.
Perfect for: Tweens, Teens, Adults
Height Restriction: 40"
Car: 4 riders per row, 8 per vehicle
Review: One of the funniest rides in the world, *The Simpsons* delivers edgy, top-quality amusement. Join Homer, Bart, Marge, Lisa, Maggie, Grampa, and the rest of Springfield as Sideshow Bob threatens to destroy Krustyland. The ride is 2D, though the characters have been rendered with 3D animation for a more immersive feel. When waiting in the queue, read as many signs as you can, as they are all filled with hilarious quips and digs at amusement park clichés.

KANG AND KODOS' TWIRL 'N' HURL

Description: Motion simulation ride starring characters from The Simpsons.
Perfect for: Young Kids and Kids

Height Restriction: None
Car: 2 riders per saucer
Review: *The Simpsons* meets Dumbo the Flying Elephant ride in this classic spin-around kid-friendly attraction. Despite the ride's name, this ride is rather slow-paced and aimed at families with young kids. Adults will get a kick out of the sound bites ripped straight from The Simpsons, though all of the humor is suitable for kids.

WOODY WOODPECKER'S KIDZONE

RIDES

E. T. ADVENTURE

Description: Ride flying bikes to help save E. T. and his home planet.
Perfect for: Families
Height Restriction: None
Car: 4 riders per row
Review: The magic of E. T. is brought to life with animatronics and rideable flying bicycles. If you've experienced Peter Pan's Flight at Disney, it's a bit like that. However, we get mixed reviews from this attraction. Tweens, teens, and young adults will likely find the ride heavily outdated. Yet, kids will love visiting E.T.'s home planet and parents will enjoy the overall nostalgia.

2024 CONSTRUCTION

Woody Woodpecker's KidZone closed in January 2023 to make room for new experiences coming to Universal Studios Florida. While Universal has yet to announce the new experiences officially, it appears that attractions based on Dreamworks (characters from various animated films are placed on the construction walls). However, the E. T. Adventure is expected to stay, as well as the SpongeBob StorePants retail location.

Ultimately, this area of the park was filled with outdated themes, including Curious George, Woody Woodpecker, and An American Tale—all franchises not as popular with kids today. So whatever Universal creates, it's expected to be kid-friendly attractions to replace the older ones.

HOLLYWOOD

SHOWS AND ATTRACTIONS

THE BOURNE STUNTACULAR

Description: A Hollywood stunt show based on *The Bourne Identity* film series.
Perfect for: Tweens, Teens, Adults
Review: A jaw-dropping indoor stunt show based on *The Bourne Identity* film series. Unlike any other stunt show before it, The Bourne Stuntacular uses a massive screen and amazing technical effects to bring the action to life!

UNIVERSAL ORLANDO'S HORROR MAKE-UP SHOW

Description: Learn how Hollywood make-up artists create movie monsters.
Perfect for: Tweens, Teens, Adults
Review: Horror movies come to life in this unique Hollywood make-up show. While there are more laughs than screams, it still may be too scary for young kids.

UNIVERSAL ORLANDO'S CINEMATIC CELEBRATION

Description: A fantastic nighttime water show with special effects and characters from *Jurassic World*, *Harry Potter*, *Despicable Me* and more.
Perfect for: Everyone
Review: This stunning, 20-minute water show brings movies to life with music and projections on water fountains in the

center lagoon. Scenes from popular film franchises are projected onto the water with music and colors. This effect looks a bit like the Bellagio Fountains in Las Vegas or the World of Color show at the Disneyland Resort in California. Cinematic Celebration brings to life the best experiences in the parks with thrilling *Harry Potter* sequences, hilarious *Despicable Me* vignettes, and a roaring *Jurassic World* segment. We highly recommend planning this show as a conclusion to your day.

> **· Magic Tips ·**
> Showtimes vary throughout the year and depend on park hours and sunset times. We recommend arriving at least 40 minutes before showtime for a better view of the water features. The key is to sit back far enough in the seating section to see all of the projections around the theme park, but close enough for the best view of the water features. The best viewings are in the center of the tiered seating area, but the show can be viewed from anywhere around the lagoon.

TRIBUTE STORE

Universal Studios Hollywood has one of the coolest stores in Orlando. The Tribute Store changes seasonally and offers different experiences with amazing props, several well-decorated rooms, and special merchandise. Past themes have included Christmas, Jurassic World, and Halloween.

DIAGON ALLEY

Later on, we detail the attractions of Diagon Alley in our Wizarding World of Harry Potter chapter.

CHAPTER FIVE

UNIVERSAL'S ISLANDS OF ADVENTURE PARK

THEMED AREAS

Islands of Adventure creates fantastic worlds based around popular franchises. From Marvel Comics and Harry Potter to Jurassic Park and Dr. Seuss, there's something for everyone at this theme park! The lands aren't actual islands placed in the middle of water. Instead, the stunning landscaping and center lake give the feeling of distinct and unique worlds separated by a body of water. However, most "islands" are connected by land.

Port of Entry

A hodgepodge of world bazaars that will make you feel like Aladdin or Indiana Jones might live there. The Port of Entry is a fun, shop-filled starting area before you step into the islands.

Marvel Super Hero Island

Islands of Adventure does justice to comic books by bringing Spider-Man, Hulk, X-Men, and other superheroes to life in this colorful area. These aren't the newer versions of Marvel's creations, but more the '80s and '90s comic book style. Thrill riders will love the high-speed Hulk Coaster and everyone will enjoy the action-packed Amazing Adventures of Spider-Man.

Note: But, doesn't Disney own Marvel? Yes, they do, but Universal acquired the rights before Disney purchased the brand.

Seuss Landing

The bright, cheerful world of Dr. Seuss awaits guests in this island designed for young kids. See The Cat in the Hat, try green eggs and ham, and ride above Circus McGurkus on a train. One of the coolest features of Seuss Landing are the wacky palm trees that were picked for their naturally bent trunks.

Toon Lagoon

Splash into the world of classic cartoons like Pop Eye, Dudley Do-Right, and Betty Boop in this vibrant island. Toon Lagoon might get overshadowed by Harry Potter and Marvel, but it's water-based attractions and attention to detail are some of the park's best.

The Lost Continent

Before Harry Potter took over, The Lost Continent was the largest island. Though its number of attractions has been significantly reduced because of Harry Potter, this mythology-themed island still has some stunning sights and delicious eats. The Lost Continent is the only island not themed after an existing franchise.

Jurassic Park

This tropical-feeling island is perfectly set as an homage to the *Jurassic Park* film series. Meet velociraptors or plunge down the river cruise after escaping a giant T-Rex. There are also many attractions for kids at the Jurassic Park Discovery Center and Camp Jurassic playground.

Skull Island

Based around Peter Jackson's *King Kong* film, this island houses one attraction: Reign of Kong. The creepy exterior of this island is filled with black rock and human skulls.

Hogsmeade – The Wizarding World of Harry Potter

The magic of *Harry Potter* comes to life in this wizard-themed wonderland. With snow-capped buildings, enchanted storefronts, and unique attractions, *Harry Potter* fans may never want to leave. Guests can enter Hogwarts Castle and purchase wands that interact with areas of Hogsmeade and Diagon Alley. Though Hogsmeade is often crowded, this island is not to be missed!

MARVEL SUPER HERO ISLAND

RIDES

DOCTOR DOOM'S FEARFALL

Description: An 18-story free-fall ride.
Perfect for: Thrill Riders
Height Restriction: 52"
Car: 4 riders per row
Single Rider Available
Review: Try and calm your nerves before facing Dr. Doom's revenge for you and The Fantastic Four. Smoke, lights, and a massive drop will make any heart race! Basically, a glorified carnival ride, but still a lot of fun. While you're at the top, there's an amazing view of the park. But what goes up must come down! We only recommend this attraction for thrill riders.

STORM FORCE ACCELATRON

Description: A spinning ride (similar to Disney's tea cups).
Perfect for: Kids, Tweens
Height Restriction: None
Car: Up to 4 riders per cup

Review: Battle Magneto alongside Storm from X-Men. Storm Force is dizzying fun for families with kids—and strong stomachs. Riders control the speed of the spinning by turning a wheel.

· Magic Tips ·
Artist Adam Kubert drew most of the 90s-inspired comics around this land. However, he wasn't allowed to traditionally sign his name on the artwork. However, he was allowed to hid his signature on within the art. Can you see where Kubert signed his name? Hint: Look on the hands of the comic book characters.

THE INCREDIBLE HULK COASTER

Description: A fast-launching steel roller coaster with loops
Type: Roller Coaster.
Perfect for: Thrill Riders
Height Restriction: 54"
Car: 4 riders in each row
Single Rider Available
Review: The Incredible Hulk Coaster was revamped in 2016 to include a new storyline and special effects. Prepare for 7 loops, high speeds, and a lot of thrilling fun! In our opinion, The Hulk Coaster is one of the best.

Note: The ride does not permit loose items such as hats, sunglasses, or cell phones in pockets. You must store these items in a locker during the ride.

THE AMAZING ADVENTURES OF SPIDER-MAN

Description: A 3-D motion simulation ride with a moving car.
Perfect for: Kids, Tweens, Teens, Adults, Thrill Riders
Height Restriction: 40"
Car: 4 riders per row
Single Rider Available

Review: Grab your 3D glasses for this motion simulator based around the many adventures of Spider-Man. Combat villains like Dr. Octopus and Hobgoblin as you race through New York City. This ride is great fun for everyone with its unique style of large screens and a moving vehicle—only the Transformers ride feels very similar.

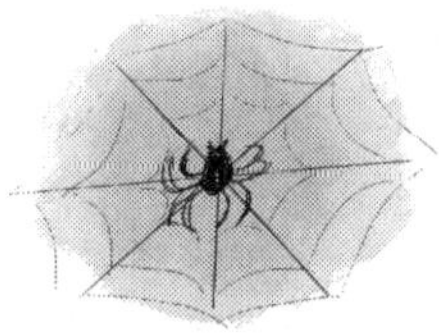

SHOWS AND ATTRACTIONS

MARVEL HEROES

Look out for members of the Avengers and the X-Men as they walk or drive through Marvel Super Hero Island. There are also meet ups with Spider-Man, Wolverine, Captain America, and other famous superheroes.

· Magic Tips ·
There are several interactive elements around Marvel Super Hero Island including telephones to hear from favorite heroes. Look for these phones and pick them up for a surprise!

SEUSS LANDING

RIDES

THE CAT IN THE HAT

Description: A slow-paced ride starring The Cat in the Hat.
Type: Dark Ride
Perfect for: Kids
Height Restriction: 36”
Car: 2-3 riders in each row

Review: Hop aboard a slow-moving car that takes you through the story of *The Cat in the Hat*. Families with kids under 10 will love the colorful scenes and crazy animatronics. Actually, *any* Dr. Seuss fan will find this ride very charming.

THE HIGH IN THE SKY SEUSS TROLLEY TRAIN RIDE

Description: A slow-moving train that winds around Seuss Landing.
Perfect for: Families
Height Restriction: 40"
Car: 2 riders per row
Review: Travel over the low buildings of Seuss Landing on this colorful train. It's a nice time if you're looking for a break, as the lines are rarely long. However, not much happens other than some sights that you can see from down below.

CARO-SEUSS-EL

Description: A Dr. Seuss-themed carousel.
Perfect for: Young Kids and Kids
Height Restriction: None
Car: 1 rider per "horse"
Review: Hop on bobbing yaks, elephants, and other Seuss-drawn creatures. Another well-detailed ride designed for families with young kids.

ONE FISH, TWO FISH, RED FISH, BLUE FISH

Description: A fish-themed ride like Dumbo the Flying Elephant at Disneyland and The Magic Kingdom.
Perfect for: Young Kids and Kids
Height Restriction: None
Car: 2 riders per fish
Review: Gently soar above the water on your choice of primary-colored fish. Control how high—or low—your fish goes! Young kids will especially love this attraction.

SHOWS AND ATTRACTIONS

OH THE STORIES YOU'LL HEAR

Description: Live stage show.
Perfect for: Families
Review: Listen to stories told by Dr. Seuss characters. Look for The Cat in the Hat, Thing 1 and Thing 2, and even the grumpy Grinch! The theatre is outdoors, but the seating area is shaded. This is perfect for families who need a break and want to watch a show.

IF I RAN THE ZOO

A hedge maze with interactive walls and water play areas. There aren't any real animals in this zoo, but kids 10 and under will love to cool off in this colorful play area.

TOON LAGOON

RIDES

DUDLEY DO-RIGHT'S RIPSAW FALLS

Description: A water flume ride starring characters from Rocky and Bullwinkle's Dudley Do-Right cartoon.
Perfect for: Kids, Tweens, Teens, Adults
Height Restriction: 44"
Car: 5 riders per log
Review: Journey through the wacky tale of Canada's cartoon Mountie on a log raft that holds five riders. At the end, you'll plunge down a seven-story waterfall. We love Dudley Do-Right's Ripsaw Falls for the beautiful decorations and comedic storytelling. This attraction is especially popular in the summer, so visit just before noon to avoid the longer lines. You will get wet, but likely not nearly as soaked as Popeye and Bluto's Bilge-Rat Barges.

POPEYE AND BLUTO'S BILGE-RAT BARGES

Description: A water rapids raft ride with the characters from Popeye cartoons.

Type: River rapids raft ride

Perfect for: Kids, Tweens, Teens, Adults

Height Restriction: 42"

Car: 12 riders per raft with seats in pairs of 2

Review: Rush down a raging rapid on rafts as Popeye and Bluto battle for Olive Oyl's attention. This is one of the best rapids rides we've ever experienced with its comical humor and cartoon design. Be prepared because you *will* get wet! We recommend experiencing this attraction in the middle of the day when the sun is shining to help you dry off.

Note: This attraction may close an hour before the park.

SHOWS AND ATTRACTIONS

ME SHIP, THE OLIVE

Popeye's 3-story ship and water play area. If you don't want to get soaked on the raft ride, there are water cannons on Me Ship, The Olive where you can take aim at riders while staying dry. Kids ages 10 and under will enjoy this play area the most.

SKULL ISLAND

RIDES

SKULL ISLAND: REIGN OF KONG

Description: A 3D journey into the island ruled by the giant gorilla, King Kong.

Type: 3D simulation ride
Perfect for: Tweens, Teens, and Adults
Height Restriction: 36"
Car: 6 riders per row
Virtual Line Pass: Yes (sometimes)
Review: Step into a dark, foreboding temple that houses a fierce, massive gorilla. A safari truck takes you into Kong's world where dinosaurs and giant spiders might attack at any moment. The ride is divided into segments, including one with a 3-D screen that domes over the caravan. In the queue, there are a few spooky surprises as well. At the end, prepare to face Kong himself. Though the special effects and animatronics are fairly impressive in this attraction, some of the storytelling elements feel repetitive compared to other rides within Universal Orlando. This attraction may be too terrifying for young kids.

THE LOST CONTINENT

SHOWS AND ATTRACTIONS

THE MYSTICAL FOUNTAIN

A sassy fountain that interacts with guests walking close to it. Step too close and you might get sprayed!

JURASSIC PARK

RIDES

JURASSIC PARK RIVER ADVENTURE

Description: A water-based boat ride with dinosaurs and an 85-foot drop.
Type: Boat ride
Perfect for: Thrill Riders
Height Restriction: 42"
Car: 4 riders per row with 5 rows per boat
Review: A boat ride that begins with gentle, animatronic giants and concludes with attacking carnivores. Drift calmly at first until the raptors and T-Rex show their teeth, then get ready for the big, eight-story fall! You'll likely get wet, but it'll be worth it because Jurassic Park River Adventure is one of the best rides in Islands of Adventure!

PTERANODON FLYERS

Description: High-flying kids' gliders on a track.
Type: Track glider
Perfect for: Kids
Height Restriction: 36" minimum (under 48" must have guardian ride, too)
Car: 2 riders per glider
Review: Kids soar around Jurassic Park island on these high-up tracked gliders. Pteranodon Flyers have a limited rider occupancy, so lines often back up. Luckily, Universal started a Virtual Line for this attraction. A kiosk in front of the ride distributes return times so your kids can have fun in the playground instead of waiting in a long line.

> **Note:** Since this attraction is designed for kids, adults must have a child between 36" and 48" with them to ride.

JURASSIC WORLD VELOCICOASTER

Description: A high-speed, dino-themed rollercoaster.

Type: Roller Coaster
Perfect for: Thrill Riders
Height Restriction: 51"
Car: 2 riders in each row
Single Rider Available
Review: The wildest ride in the park! The Jurassic World VelociCoaster is a smooth, high-speed coaster with several inversions—and airtime! Yes, you will lift out of your seat on this ride! Designed for those looking for thrills, the VelociCoaster also has a great queue filled with Jurassic movie Easter eggs and animatronics. If you just want to see the queue, there's an indoor waiting area just before the coaster launches. All items must be stored inside of a free locker before riding. You'll see the locker in the queue before you board.

SHOWS AND ATTRACTIONS

RAPTOR ENCOUNTER

Visit the Jurassic World Raptor Paddock and meet Blue the Velociraptor. A "keeper" will explain raptor behaviors and you can even pose for a terrifying photo with the dinosaur! You can also meet other dinosaurs in the area including the adorable Sierra, the baby velociraptor!

> **· Magic Tips ·**
> The dinosaurs in the Raptor Encounter take turns throughout the hour. Typically, the first 40 minutes of the hour is Blue's spot and the last 20 minutes is Baby Sierra's.

CAMP JURASSIC

An outdoor play area for kids to run, play, swing, and jump. The design is like an archeological dig site where kids can squirt each other with water cannons and play in giant nets surrounded by lush trees.

HOGSMEADE VILLAGE

We detail Hogsmeade Village and the rest of the Wizarding World of Harry Potter in the next chapter.

CHAPTER SIX

THE WIZARDING WORLD OF HARRY POTTER

INTRODUCTION

In May of 2007, Universal Orlando announced a new realm of themed entertainment for its guests. The Wizarding World would take visitors into the magical adventures of the *Harry Potter* films. There, they'd fly through Hogwarts Castle, shop in hotspots around Hogsmeade Village, and even drink the famous Butterbeer! After opening in June of 2010, the Wizarding World of Harry Potter did not disappoint eager Harry Potter fans from around the world. There are rides, thrills, and seemingly real magic for all to enjoy! Best of all, the land feels totally real. It's like stepping into the Harry Potter series and living your own unforgettable adventure.

The announcement of Harry Potter also meant the departure of some previous attractions. Half of the popular Lost Continent land in Islands of Adventure was transformed into Hogsmeade Village, and even the original Flying Unicorn roller coaster was reimagined into the current Flight of the Hippogriff. In Universal Studios Florida, the classic Jaws water ride closed to make way for Diagon Alley.

It's no secret that the Harry Potter attractions are some of Universal Orlando's biggest crowd-bringers. Both of the parks (Universal Studios Florida and Universal's Islands of Adventure) have their own *Harry Potter*-themed lands. Islands of Adventure has the original Hogsmeade Village with the towering Hogwarts Castle, Ollivanders Wand Shop, Honeydukes candy store, and Three Broomsticks restaurant. Diagon Alley, found in the Universal Studios Florida park, has Gringotts bank, a second Ollivanders Wand Shop, and even Knockturn Alley, where guests can explore the darker side of magic.

Author J. K. Rowling is one of the creative forces behind these lands, making the Wizarding World feel authentic. A visit to the Wizarding World of Harry Potter is difficult to describe. There are sights, smells, and sounds for every sense. The smoking, rustic buildings of Diagon Alley are stunning and the fire-breathing dragon perched atop Gringotts bank is jaw dropping. Even the actors from the Harry Potter films make appearances on the rides!

In this chapter, we review the attractions and shops, as well as give tips for exploring the Wizarding World of Harry Potter. It's like visiting a theme park within another theme park, and truly, there's nothing else like it!

HOGSMEADE VILLAGE

In the *Harry Potter* novels, Hogsmeade Village is a town just outside of the grounds of Hogwarts Castle. Most of the architecture is designed after 17-century Scottish villages with granite stone and steeped roofs. In Orlando, the rooftops and thin chimneys are covered in glistening white snow all year long.

Traditionally, Hogsmeade is reserved for students third year and higher (ages 13 and older). Once they've reached this age, they can venture into the village to shop and dine as they please. The remote Hogsmeade Village is the only town in all of Great Britain that's completely occupied by wizarding folk. Though there's a great lake and some forested areas between Hogwarts and Hogsmeade in the books, guests are just steps away from the famous castle at the theme park. Hogwarts is huge, stunning, and picturesque. It's a great place to stop for a selfie and you can even explore its grounds while in the queue for the Harry Potter and the Forbidden Journey attraction!

There are currently three rides in Hogsmeade Village: Harry Potter and the Forbidden Journey, Flight of the Hippogriff, and Hagrid's Magical Creatures Motorbike Adventure. While all are family-oriented attractions, younger kids will enjoy the Flight of the Hippogriff junior coaster more than they might Hagrid's thrilling coaster ride. However, each contains unique Harry Potter storytelling for fans of all ages.

Outside of the rides, there's still plenty to do. Several shops, snack spots, and a dining location make up the bulk of Hogsmeade Village. Ollivanders Wand Shop is a show where one lucky visitor will become a witch or wizard as a wand chooses them! In fact, it's not uncommon to see robed guests zipping down the streets of Hogsmeade, brandishing wands to use in several locations around the land. Each wand comes with a map for Hogsmeade and Diagon Alley, illustrating locations where their wand can cast "spells" that interact with the Wizarding World! There are countless ways to enjoy Hogsmeade, and we lay them out for you in this next section.

RIDES

HARRY POTTER AND THE FORBIDDEN JOURNEY

Description: An adventure ride starring the characters of the *Harry Potter* films.
Type: Simulation ride
Perfect for: Kids, Tweens, Teens, and Adults
Height Restriction: 48" (122 cm)
Car: 4 riders per row
Virtual Line Pass: Yes
Single Rider Available
Review: Enter the magnificent Hogwarts Castle and meet Harry Potter characters in the various rooms. Look for enchanted portraits, magic spells, a winding garden, and stunning artwork. The queue is just as entertaining as the ride. Once you board a specialized crane-like vehicle, you'll fly through Hogwarts to encounter a game of Quidditch, a run-away dragon, spitting spiders, and even soul-sucking Dementors. Harry Potter and the Forbidden Journey is one of the most unique rides in the world, and not to be missed!

⋆ Magic Tips ⋆

You must store your loose items in a locker before riding Harry Potter and the Forbidden Journey. These are near the attraction's queue.

This ride can make some guests with motion sickness feel very ill. Also, there is a "haunted house" style to this attraction with creeping spiders and scary Dementors. Small children, even those tall enough to ride, may feel frightened.

If you're worried about your comfort on the ride, a test seat is available before the queue.

HAGRID'S MAGICAL CREATURES MOTORBIKE ADVENTURE

Description: Wind through the Forbidden Forest on this story-based rollercoaster with cinematic scenes, animatronic magical creatures, and beautiful forested scenery.
Type: Roller coaster
Perfect for: Kids, Tweens, Teens, Adults, Thrill Riders
Height Restriction: 48" (122 cm)
Car: 2 riders per row with motorbike and sidecar seats
Virtual Line Pass: Yes
Single Rider Sometimes Available
Review: Hagrid's Magical Creatures Motorbike Adventure is a nearly 3-minute long journey of fantastic Harry Potter storytelling. There are animatronics, stop-and-go zips, and even surprising drops! Riders sit side by side on a motorbike-style coaster with sidecar or bike seat options. Each seat provides a different experience. The driver's seat has a thrilling motorbike feel while the sidecar is similar to a classic roller coaster (though larger riders will feel more comfortable with the less-cramped driver's seat). You may have to wait a while for this coaster, but it's well worth your time!

⋆ Magic Tips ⋆

You must store your loose items in a locker before riding Hagrid's Magical Creatures Motorbike Adventure. These are provided in the queue of the attraction.

1,000 trees were planted to create the Forbidden Forest that surrounds Hagrid's Motorbike Adventure! There are also several Harry Potter-related surprises within the queue that you won't want to miss!

The Forbidden Forest really comes to life at night. If you can, ride both in the daytime and the darkness for an entirely different feel.

FLIGHT OF THE HIPPOGRIFF

Description: An outdoor junior roller coaster.

Type: Junior roller coaster
Perfect for: Young Kids, Kids, Tweens
Height Restriction: 36"
Car: 2 riders per row

Review: A hippogriff is half eagle, half horse and very moody. Hagrid, the groundskeeper at Hogwarts castle, once had a hippogriff named Buckbeak who befriends Harry Potter. This ride is inspired by that creature. Flight of the Hippogriff is a great introductory roller coaster for kids who need a stepping stone to the bigger coasters. Though the ride is just over a minute in length, the track is smooth and fun for the whole family.

> **Note:** The seats on this ride are designed for kids, so taller and larger guests may not sit comfortably in them. Unfortunately, Flight of the Hippogriff does not offer a test seat.

HOGWARTS EXPRESS

Travel between Islands of Adventure and Universal Studios on the famous train from Harry Potter. You'll need a park-to-park ticket to ride. The experiences are different, depending if you travel to or from Hogsmeade. For more details about the Hogwarts Express, see Diagon Alley in the Universal Studios chapter.

SHOWS

OLLIVANDERS

Description: An intimate, 7-minute show where the wand chooses the wizard!
Perfect for: Harry Potter fans of all ages

Review: Located next to the famous Ollivanders--where Harry Potter gets his wand—this show isn't to be missed by any Wizarding World fan. Garrick Ollivander, or one of his assistants, invites a lucky park guest to take part in the wand selection experience. Only around 24 guests see the show at a time, so the line can get quite long for the brief experience. Still, we think that Ollivanders is one of the better shows at Universal for its magical and emotional storytelling sure to touch the hearts of all that experience it. Sadly, only one person per group gets chosen for a wand experience and keeping the wand costs full price (around $55). There is a nearly identical version of this show in Diagon Alley.

> **⋆ Magic Tips ⋆**
> There isn't a surefire way to be chosen by Ollivander, but from what we've noticed, participants usually near the front and to his right get picked the most. Though there are always exceptions, he mostly chooses guests who appear between ages 8-20.

THE NIGHTTIME LIGHTS AT HOGWARTS CASTLE

One of the best shows at Universal Orlando is projected onto the Hogwarts Castle on select summer nights. This brief, 5-minute show runs about every 20 minutes in front of the castle.

THE DARK ARTS AT HOGWARTS CASTLE

Similar to the Nighttime Lights at Hogwarts Castle, this seasonal projection show covers the dark side of the Wizarding World. Projections display wicked curses, creatures, and even fantastic magic brought to life in mind-blowing ways!

> **⋆ Magic Tips ⋆**
> Viewing the Nighttime Lights or The Dark Arts at Hogwarts Castle may be difficult due to limited space. We recommend getting a times guide when you enter the park (near the maps) and arriving 20 minutes before showtime.
>
> After sundown, the only way into Hogsmeade is through The Lost Continent, as the projection show

prohibits guests flowing in from Jurassic Park Island—though exiting is possible. The best viewing spots are near Flight of the Hippogriff or the small stage where the Frog Choir and Triwizard Spirit Rally perform.

THE FROG CHOIR

See Hogwarts students and their singing toads perform songs from the Wizarding World. The singers are talented and the show runs about 10 minutes.

TRIWIZARD SPIRIT RALLY

See wizard students from foreign wizarding schools,Durmstrang and Beauxbatons show their school spirit with dazzling choreographed routines. The show runs about 5 minutes and is a lot of fun to watch while sipping on Butterbeer.

WAND SPOTS

Wands purchased at Ollivanders come with a map of the various magic practice locations around Hogsmeade Village. In these spots, guests can test spells by moving their wand in specific directions. These movements trigger several magical happenings around Hogsmeade Village and Diagon Alley.

DINING

Food is one of the best parts of the Harry Potter book series and the Wizarding World is no different! We recommend trying some of the delicious sweets and eats around the lands—you might find something that amazes you.

THREE BROOMSTICKS

Description: Dine in Hogsmeade Village's traditional eatery. There are plenty of signature British dishes and snacks to try. Three Broomsticks is our favorite quick-service dining spot in the Universal Orlando Resort for its delicious food, themed dining, and large portions!

Type: Quick-Service (Lunch and Dinner)
Price: $$
Reservations: No
Menu Items: fish and chips, Cornish pasties, spare ribs, chicken, turkey leg, salads, shepherd's pie, Butterbeer, *Harry Potter*-themed desserts

THREE BROOMSTICKS RECOMMENDATIONS

- **Fish and Chips (entree)** - Battered and fried fish served with thick-cut french fries and tartar sauce.

- **Spare Ribs Platter (entree)** - Pork ribs coated in tangy barbecue sauce and served with husked corn and roasted potatoes.

- **Shepherd's Pie with Garden Salad (entree)** - Flaky meat pie with beef, lamb, cooked veggies, and topped with mashed potatoes—served with a garden salad and choice of dressing.

- **Butterbeer Potted Cream (dessert)** - Smooth butterscotch-flavored pudding with a dollop of whipped cream.

⋆ Magic Tips ⋆

If you're planning on lunch at Three Broomsticks on a busy day, we recommend getting there by 11:30am to avoid the lunch rush. For later lunching, head there after 2:30pm. Dinner at Three Broomsticks isn't as popular as midday dining.

HOG'S HEAD

Description: Located in the back of Three Broomsticks restaurant, the Hog's Head is a famous Wizarding World pub from the books and film. There are delicious drinks here for guests of all ages and alcoholic beverages for those over 21. The bartenders are usually very friendly and can help you decide which drink to purchase. Behind the bar is a moving hog head that's magically brought to life!

Type: Bar

Price: $-$$

Reservations: No

Drinks: Butterbeer (soda, frozen, and hot), Pumpkin Juice, Gillywater, mixed drinks, beers, wine

HOG'S HEAD RECOMMENDATIONS

- **Dragonscale Ale (alcoholic beverage)** - An amber lager with caramel malt flavors.
- **Pear Dazzle (alcoholic beverage)** - A fruity mixed drink with vodka, pear cider, lemonade, and a cherry on top!
- **Hog's Head Brew (alcoholic beverage)** - A mild, smooth red ale with a small "hop" and tangy taste.
- **Fishy Green Ale (nonalcoholic beverage)** - A mint and cinnamon drink with tart blueberry-flavored "fish egg" pearls.
- **Tongue Tying Lemon Squash (nonalcoholic beverage)** - A refreshing lemonade with a fresh and lightly sweet taste.
- **Peachtree Fizzing Tea (nonalcoholic beverage)** - A lightly sweet iced tea with peach and ginger flavors.

• Magic Tips •

The Hog's Head Brew is a popular beer only served at the Hog's Head in Hogsmeade Village!

There's a secret menu item served at the Hog's Head called The Triple—or the Deathly Hallows. It's an alcoholic drink with cider, Hog's Head Brew, and Guinness. It's a nice treat for beer lovers looking for some extra adventure in their drink!

THE BEST SNACKS AND DRINKS

BUTTERBEER – A delicious, non-alcoholic butterscotch soda served with a whipped cream topping. Butterbeer comes as a traditional soda or a less sweet frozen (slushy) version. Find it at the Butterbeer carts in both Harry Potter lands, Hog's Head, Three Broomsticks, and the Leaky Cauldron. Butterbeer also comes in a "hot" form which is served sort of like a rich and creamy latte. This is great for cold and rainy days (as rare as they might be in Orlando).

• Magic Tips •

Three Broomsticks also serves a vegan version of Butterbeer that tastes very similar to the original! You can order it at Three Broomsticks and Leaky Cauldron.

We love mixing the Hog's Head Brew (beer) with Butterbeer (if you're 21 years or older). It's not for everyone, but if you enjoy sweeter beers, this makes for a great combination! You'll have to order them separately and try them together.

CHOCOLATE FROG – A deliciously creamy, solid milk chocolate frog. Each frog comes with a holographic collectable card featuring a famous wizard! Get these at Honeydukes. Makes a great gift to take home!

BUTTERBEER FUDGE – An ultra-sweet bar of creamy butterscotch flavor. Get this treat at Honeydukes in Hogsmeade Village and Sugarplums in Diagon Alley.

NO-MELT ICE CREAM – Served like traditional ice cream in a variety of flavors—like chocolate, vanilla, and even pumpkin—this delicious treat isn't ice cream at all. Instead, it's similar to whipped cream which means that it won't melt even on the hottest day. Find it at Honeydukes in Hogsmeade Village and Sugarplums in Diagon Alley.

PUMPKIN PASTIES – A flaky, pumpkin pie-flavored pastry. Pumpkin Pasties can be purchased at Honeydukes in Hogsmeade Village and Sugarplums in Diagon Alley.

PUMPKIN JUICE – This nonalcoholic drink comes in a very cool bottle with a pumpkin-shaped cap. The flavor is a swirl of apple juice, pumpkin puree, sugar, and other fruity flavors. It seems that there's a dash of nutmeg and other spices that sort of make this cold, sweet drink taste like a Christmas beverage. We highly recommend trying pumpkin juice, especially for those with a sweet tooth. Get it at carts around Hogsmeade Village and Diagon Alley.

Note: Many of the snack carts sell bottles of Gillywater. While this drink looks interesting, it's nothing more than typical bottled water with a fancy, *Harry Potter*-themed label (in the books and films, the similarly named gillyweed gave Harry Potter the ability to breath underwater). If you're looking to get creative with your Gillywater, stop by the Eternelle's Elixir of Refreshment stand in Diagon Alley for mix-in "potions" that add flavor to these bottles!

SHOPPING

DERVISH AND BANGES – Think of this store as the gift shop of Hogsmeade Village. Get everything from t-shirts to broomsticks here to take home! Dervish and Banges is also a great spot for getting Hogwarts House-related items like Gryffindor and Slytherin goods. All of the merchandise is beautifully crafted to appease even the most scrutinizing Harry Potter fan. Of course, this also means that the prices are fairly high for some of the goods. We recommend setting aside a budget before visiting.

⋆ Magic Tips ⋆

Everything in Dervish and Banges—as well as the rest of the Wizarding World of Harry Potter—is designed to appear authentic to the story. This means that you'll be able to find merchandise and apparel that Harry Potter could have purchased himself. For that reason, you won't find a t-shirt that reads "The Wizarding World of Harry Potter" here. For those, you'll need to purchase at stores outside of the Wizarding World.

Have you ever been sorted into a Harry Potter house? If not, we recommend visiting **WizardingWorld.com**, the official website for all things Harry Potter. Sign up for a free account to discover your Hogwarts House and other magical designations. Then, once you arrive in Hogsmeade Village, you'll know which of the schools you belong to for merchandise purchases!

FILCH'S EMPORIUM OF CONFISCATED GOODS - Get school supplies based on the houses of Hogwarts and more. There are also toys, robes, and even cases filled with neat Harry Potter artifacts that aren't for sale—including a Marauder's Map with footsteps moving about the paper!

HONEYDUKES – Pick out your choice of sweet on seemingly endless shelves of candy. We recommend checking out the baked goods counter for some extra-delicious dessert options.

OWL POST – Take home an owl stuffed animal or mail parcels and letters to loved ones from this unique location. Friends and family love receiving packages stamped with the Hogsmeade seal.

SECRETS OF HOGSMEADE VILLAGE

He-Who-Must-Not-Be-Named – Some of the team members working in the Wizarding World do not enjoy hearing Voldemort's name. Have a little fun with them and mention him to see what they say!

A Familiar Voice – In the restrooms, listen for the voice of Moaning Myrtle as she giggles in the pipes!

Free Elf – In Three Broomsticks, look near the ceiling for Dobby's shadow! He seems to be practicing magic for a certain wizard boy.

Cool Witchcraft – In the queue for Harry Potter and the Forbidden Journey, stick around in the Dark Arts room to see Hermione magically pour snow all over the room!

Dropping By – Look up toward the ceiling in the Owl Post and you'll see the birds hooting above. Look down and you'll see their mess, so watch your step!

You're in Trouble Now! – When a wizard or witch has misbehaved, they might receive an angry-voiced letter called a Howler. Outside the Owl Post, you can see a Howler appear on a certain spot to scream at you!

Cuckowl Clock – Every now and then you'll see an owl pop out of a small door atop the Owlery!

Little Headed – To the left of the hog's head (in its pub), look for three shrunken heads. These are from the movie *Harry Potter and the Prisoner of Azkaban*!

More in Store – Harry Potter fanatics may want to explore Hogsmeade for additional storefronts. There are several windows to stores (that cannot be entered) including Madam Puddifoot's Teas & Cakes!

DIAGON ALLEY

As fantastic as Hogsmeade Village is, Diagon Alley is somehow even more stunning. The location is hidden from plain sight, but guests can follow the breadcrumbs (or other visitors walking though a wall) to enter Diagon Alley. A breathtaking view opens before you with dingy railways above and a formidable fire-breathing dragon in the distance! The details from the paint colors to the individual grooves on storefronts make this a beautifully artistic place.

Many of the same attractions like dining, shopping, and a second Ollivanders reside in Diagon Alley as they do Hogsmeade Village. However, the shops of Diagon have a much darker tone, like a seedy alley in London. Even seedier is Knockturn Alley, a place for dark artifacts in the depths of this land. Here, guests can purchase merchandise to make wicked witches and wizards proud.

In the books and films, Diagon Alley is the first place where Harry Potter sees the Wizarding World come to life. He's given money from Gringotts bank to purchase clothes, school supplies, and a wand from Diagon Alley. You, too, can create your own Wizarding World adventure by visiting many of these same destinations!

Diagon Alley opened with two rides: Harry Potter and the Escape from Gringotts and the Hogwarts Express. Gringotts takes place in the bank of the same name where treacherous wizards have threatened to steal valuables from it. Harry Potter and the gang team up to save the day—and the guests from danger!

The Hogwarts Express is the only ride in Universal Orlando that requires a Park-to-Park ticket. This gentle ride takes guests from Universal Studios Florida to Islands of Adventure with some fun Harry Potter storytelling. The queue for the ride is actually outside and to the left of Diagon Alley in King's Cross Station.

Just like in Hogsmeade, Diagon Alley has its own set of magical wand spots, dining, snack stations, and secrets to explore!

RIDES

HARRY POTTER AND THE ESCAPE FROM GRINGOTTS

Description: A 3-D steel roller coaster starring characters from the *Harry Potter* film series.
Perfect for: Kids, Tweens, Teens, Adults, Thrill Riders
Height Restriction: 42"
Car: 4 riders per row
Virtual Line Pass: Yes
Single Rider Available
Review: Enter the cavernous vaults of Gringotts bank and ride an enchanted mine cart as you face Lord Voldemort and his evil band of Death Eaters! The visuals are stunning

beginning with the elevator that takes you into the cave-like start of the coaster. 3D glasses add to the experience as magical creatures and dark wizards attack, unleashing their fury until Harry Potter arrives to save the day! Escape from Gringotts is a great first ride, even from the details in the queue alone! While thrill riders will wish the coaster was a bit more intense, families will find the speed just right.

HOGWARTS EXPRESS

Description: A steam engine train that takes visitors from Universal Orlando to Islands of Adventure.
Perfect for: Everyone
Car: Up to 8 riders per car
Required: A Park-to-Park admission ticket
Review: Zip through the wall of Platform 9 ¾ to board the Hogwarts Express. You'll see famous characters from *Harry Potter* outside the window and face danger in this slow moving yet exciting attraction. We highly recommend this ride for every Harry Potter fan. Since the train links both parks, you will need a Park-to-Park admission ticket in order to ride.

⋆ Magic Tips ⋆

In the queue for the Hogwarts Express, look for the Platform 9 ¾ entrance. You'll see other park guests magically disappear through a wall and into the Hogwarts Express platform!

SHOWS

OLLIVANDERS

Just like in Hogsmeade Village, this is a show where the wand chooses the wizard. There are some different special effects in this experience, so you may want to see both during your visit!

THE KNIGHT BUS

Just outside of Diagon Alley is a strange, purple bus. Don't be afraid to step next to it and talk with its driver and a shrunken head. He also loves to pose for a picture!

CELESTINE WARBECK AND THE BANSHEES

The bewitching sensation sings her most famous tunes at various times. She's actually pretty good!

THE TALES OF BEEDLE THE BARD

Wizard and witch actors retell the tales of Beedle the Bard using stunning puppets. Kids will love this one!

GRINGOTTS DRAGON

The most eye-catching attraction in Diagon Alley is its resident dragon. She perches like a massive bat atop Gringotts Wizarding Bank and breathes real fire! This type of dragon is a Ukrainian Ironbelly and she's a bit temperamental!

⋆ Magic Tips ⋆

The dragon's fire blazes about every 5-15 minutes. You'll know that she's about to blow when you hear her deep, terrifying growl (though sometimes there are false alarms). Snap a photo from the center of the alley or from the side (near the golden goblin statue) to see the entire flame at once!

WAND SPOTS

Wands purchased at Ollivanders come with a map of the various practice locations around Diagon Alley. In these spots, guests can test out spells using their wands. Specific movements trigger several magical happenings. Wands work in Diagon Alley as well as Hogsmeade Village!

⋆ Magic Tips ⋆
Open your wand map in Knockturn Alley to see a special glow in certain spots!

DIAGON ALLEY DINING

Note: While Leaky Cauldron and Three Broomsticks have slightly different menus, many of the same food and drink items are found in both Hogsmeade and Diagon Alley.

LEAKY CAULDRON

Description: Dine like a witch or wizard in this stunningly detailed British restaurant. See artifacts straight from the *Harry Potter* series and savor delicious offerings inspired by the movies and books! Leaky Cauldron is one of our favorite dining spots in Universal.
Type: Quick Service
Price: $$
Reservations: No
Menu Items: fish and chips, bangers and mash, Guinness stew, fisherman's pie, toad in the hole, mini pies, chicken sandwich, *Harry Potter*-themed desserts, Butterbeer

LEAKY CAULDRON RECOMMENDATIONS

- **Fish and Chips (entree)** - Battered and fried fish served with thick-cut french fries and tartar sauce.
- **Bangers and Mash (entree)** - Pork sausages served with mashed potatoes.

- **Ploughman's (entree for 2)** - Shareable cheeses, bread, Scotch eggs, dipping sauces, and salad. Though this plate is meant for two, the portions are better for those with smaller appetites.

- **Sticky Toffee Pudding (dessert)** - A warm dessert pudding cake served with ice cream on top!

> ⋆ **Magic Tips** ⋆
> While we enjoy the Leaky Cauldron, we find that the food and scenery of Three Broomsticks is a lot better. If you have to choose between the two, we recommend heading to the dining spot in Hogsmeade Village instead.

THE HOPPING POT

This bar serves similar drinks to the Hog's Head in Hogsmeade Village. We recommend trying the Fishy Green Ale here, a nonalcoholic beverage with mint, cinnamon, and blueberry-flavored "fish egg" popping pearls. For more drink recommendations, see the previous list from the Hog's Head.

THE FOUNTAIN OF FAIR FORTUNE

A second bar in Diagon Alley with a similar selection of drinks. However, this bar usually has a much shorter line than The Hopping Pot. Guests 21 and older can also try Fire Whisky here made famous in the *Harry Potter* books. This liquor is similar to Fireball Whisky but doesn't have as strong of a kick.

FLOREAN FORTESCUE'S ICE-CREAM PARLOUR

Try some perfectly concocted ice cream flavors in this shop. There are some interesting choices here including Butterbeer, Chocolate Chili, and Apple Crumble ice cream!

ETERNELLE'S ELIXER OF REFRESHMENT

Gillywater is served at most snack carts and dining spots throughout Diagon Alley and Hogsmeade Village. It has a fancy name and even a fancy-looking bottle, but this is just regular bottled water. However, the Eternelle's Elixir of Refreshment stand sells flavor "potions" for your Gillywater! We recommend the Elixir to Induce Euphoria—a mix of pineapple, green apple, and mint flavors.

SHOPPING

KNOCKTURN ALLEY – Venture, if you dare, into the seedy passageways of Diagon Alley. See how wizards practice dark magic and, if you have a wand, attempt to cast some spells yourself!

BORGIN AND BURKES – Deep within Knockturn Alley is a dungeon-like shop for dark wizards and witches. Find some of the Wizarding World's wickedest collectables within this store.

⋆ Magic Tips ⋆

In Knockturn Alley's Borgin and Burkes, look for the Vanishing Cabinet. Listen closely and hear the tweets of a bird—likely the same one that Draco Malfoy used!

MAGICAL MENAGERIE – Adopt a magical pet (a stuffed animal or toy) in this wizarding pet store!

GRINGOTTS MONEY EXCHANGE - Bring in your "muggle money" (this means US currency) and exchange for Gringotts cash. You won't be losing out though because your Gringotts cash works in Hogsmeade and Diagon Alley to purchase goods! It's also fun to interact with the grumpy goblin who exchanges your money.

> **⋆ Magic Tips ⋆**
> Gringotts Money Exchange gives out increments of $10 and $20 banknotes. Though they are meant for the Wizarding World, this currency can also be used at select shopping spots around Universal Orlando.

WEASLEYS' WIZARD WHEEZES – Get wizarding gag gifts and other assorted fun items at this joke shop run by the Weasley brothers.

MADAM MALKIN'S ROBES FOR ALL OCCASIONS – A store with garments and accessories fit for any wizard. See collectables gathered from the Wizarding World as well as beautiful robes to wear in the parks!

QUALITY QUIDDITCH SUPPLIES – Sport your favorite house with clothing from the Harry Potter films and books. Some of these garments are activewear while others are great for lounging at home.

SCRIBBULOUS – A parchment and quill store for handlettering! We love the wax seals that can be purchased here to seal letters and packages for mailing.

SUGARPLUM'S SWEETSHOP – Try some classic wizarding treats like peppermint toads and chocolate frogs! This shop is similar to Honeydukes in Hogsmeade Village. One of our favorite gifts here are the Bertie Bott's Every-Flavor Beans. This box of jelly beans has an assortment of surprise flavors like cherry, cinnamon, or earwax!

WANDS BY GREGOROVITCH – Like at Ollivanders, this wand shop offers a wide variety of crafted wands for witches and wizards.

WISEACRE'S WIZARDING EQUIPMENT – Pick up magical collectables all around this unique store. Some of the rarer—and more expensive—items are only found here.

GLOBUS MUNDI – A small travel wizarding travel agency with t-shirts and handbags for your next trip (or your journey home).

OWL POST – Send packages home with stamps that read "Diagon Alley" on them. You can also have your items hand-wrapped for mailing starting at around $20.

⋆ **Magic Tips** ⋆

Buy too much? Don't lug all of your belongings around with you all day. Instead, have them sent to your Universal Orlando hotel room or even ship them back home! Ask your store merchant for details.

SECRETS OF DIAGON ALLEY

Grimmauld Place – Before entering Diagon Alley, look to the right for a sign that reads "Grimmauld Place." Harry Potter fans will know this as a famous spot from the books. Look at the window at 12 Grimmauld Place to see Kreacher, the grumpy house elf peeking out at guests!

Dialing Magic – The red telephone booth outside of King's Cross Station (outside of Diagon Alley) has a rotary dial phone. Dial 62442—or MAGIC—and you'll hear from the Ministry of Magic!

On-Boarding Rooming – The purple Knight Bus outside of Diagon Alley is set up for overnight guests. Of course, you can't actually sleep inside of it, but you can see the beds and other amenities from a window in the back of the bus.

Sink Your Teeth into This One – Universal pays tribute to the former Jaws attraction (where Diagon Alley now resides) in a record case in the London Record Shop window. The cover shows a circle of ladies and the title "Here's to Swimmin' with Bow Legged Women" by The Quint Trio. Quint, a character from *Jaws*, says this exact line in the movie!

A Toothy Surprise – Look behind the potted plants in the window of Florean Fortescue's Ice-Cream Parlour to see a curiously placed shark jaw (another tribute to *the Jaws* ride)!

Dripping Signs – Outside of the Leaky Cauldron, look for the sign to the shop. The cauldron actually leaks droplets of water!

How Do I Look? – There's a sassy mirror in Madam Malkin's store that gives some interesting clothing tips when you stand in front of it!

Dark Weather – When taking the Hogwarts Express from Hogsmeade to Diagon Alley, there's a scene through the window with a lightning bolt. However, if you look closely, you'll see that Voldemort is the source of the electricity!

Speaking in Tongues – In the Wizarding World, Parseltongue is a language spoken by serpents and certain wizards. The large snakes in the Magical Menagerie sometimes speak to guests in Parseltongue until you magically hear it in English!

WIZARDING WORLD CHRISTMAS

During the holiday season, the Wizarding World transforms with Christmas magic. See wreaths and other decorations adorning Diagon Alley and Hogsmeade Village. On select nights (usually around the weekends and holiday weeks), Hogwarts Castle has a special display of The Magic of Christmas, a projection show. This beautiful nighttime event is worth seeing and runs about every 20 minutes.

Special holiday snacks and sweets are found during this season in various shops. Celestina Warbeck in Diagon Alley and the Frog Choir in Hogsmeade Village perform holiday songs daily.

The holiday celebrations run from mid-November through the first week of January.

⋆ Magic Tips ⋆

The nighttime shows can become packed and team members may not allow you near the castle until after the show. The show concludes with fireworks, so once you spot these, head over for the next showing as the crowd clears.

CHAPTER SEVEN

UNIVERSAL'S VOLCANO BAY WATER PARK

INTRODUCTION

In 2017, Universal Orlando Resort opened a world-class water park styled after a Polynesian island. Volcano Bay centers around an active "volcano" that steams and houses several unique water slides. Filled with fun for young kids and thrill seekers alike, Volcano Bay lives up to Universal's aspiration for a third theme park.

Volcano Bay was built for relaxation. There's a large wave pool in the center of a steaming volcano and a lazy river that glides guests around the property. However, those looking for adventure can also find it by riding down several waterslides that plunge into the depths of the volcano!

> **Note:** Some of the slides have height and weight restrictions that will prevent some from riding. We list these restrictions in the ride descriptions.

TAPUTAPU

Volcano Bay does things differently than Universal Studios and Islands of Adventure. Most of the rides are "queue-less," meaning that you don't have to wait in a physical line to board your desired attraction. Instead, you are given a special waterproof bracelet called a TapuTapu. By scanning your bracelet on special totems near the slides, you'll have your wait time held for you. Your bracelet (which sort of looks like an old school Tamagotchi) will buzz when it's your turn to return to the slide. In the meantime, you can walk around the park and ride other water slides, lounge, eat, float in the lazy river—or do whatever else your heart desires. We suggest making plenty of relaxing time in the lazy river and wave pool for the best enjoyment of this park.

Here's What the TapuTapu Does...

1. Virtual Queue – Holds your place in line without having to actually wait in a queue
2. Locker – Store your belongings in a locker starting at $8 (prices may change) and use TapuTapu as a key
3. Photo Spots – Takes special photos near choice spots and can e-mail them to you
4. Explosions – Scan your bracelet at special spots around the Kopiko Wai Winding River and other attractions to cue explosions or control water cannons
5. Payment – Guests can link their credit card and room charges to the TapuTapu bracelet for easy ordering of food, snacks, and beverages around the park.

Note: When you first try the TapuTapu bracelet, its functionality may feel confusing, especially on crowded days. It takes about an hour to get the hang of it, so get there at park opening if you can, before the crowd rush, and start experimenting with the TapuTapu.

VOLCANO BAY EXPRESS PASS

Volcano Bay offers an Express Pass which starts around $20 per day. However, most of the busier seasons—especially during warmer weather—have prices around $70 per person, on top of the Volcano Bay day ticket. This add-on ticket allows for skipping lines to select attractions, including the popular Krakatau Aqua Coaster which can have a wait time of up to 3 hours on busy days. The water park also has an Express Pass PLUS option for more attractions, though we don't find this as necessary as the other pass.

The standard Express Pass gets one skip-the-line entry for 8 attractions and the Express Pass PLUS allows for skipping 12 attractions. The price difference between the two is usually around $30.

We only recommend Express Pass at Volcano Bay if you aren't planning on visiting the park at opening or are going during the busy season. For example, if the park opens at 10am on a Friday in August, but you're arriving around 12pm, it's a great idea to purchase an Express Pass to maximize your experience. Otherwise, arrive before the park opens and experience the popular Krakatau Aqua Coaster first to save time waiting.

· Magic Tips ·

The Express Pass PLUS for Volcano Bay often sells out before the day of visit. If you are planning on purchasing this pass, make sure you do so weeks before your arrival.

WHAT TO BRING

The water parks have nearly everything you'll need for poolside fun—but with a cost. That's why we recommend bringing these items with you into the parks:

1. Sunscreen – You'll be out in the sun all day, after all.
2. Beach towels – Rentals are available.
3. Change of clothing – It's not required, but good to have if you plan to go somewhere afterward.

· Magic Tips ·

Volcano Bay does not allow glass, coolers, your own rafts, or life vests into the park (they provide complimentary life vests if needed). You also cannot wear shoes onto the rides, though rash guards and water shirts are allowed. If you wear sunglasses, be careful not to lose them on a water slide!

Money-Saving Tips
Volcano Bay allows guests to bring their own snacks into the park and bottled water. To save some money, we recommend packing some of these for your visit.

CABANAS AND LOUNGERS

Looking for a reserved spot out of the sun? Volcano Bay's cabanas are a perfect addition for your trip. Starting at $29.99, you and your family can enjoy a reserved spot in the shade.

Having a cabana makes a trip to Volcano Bay much easier than without one. First, you won't have to find a set of chairs for your traveling party and you'll also have a place to put your things. There's also lots of shade from the constant Central Florida sun during the warmest months.

However, cabanas aren't cheap. The largest ones can cost hundreds of dollars, thus increasing the total cost of your one-day visit to a water park. Really, parents with young kids and those wishing to lounge for most of the day benefit from the cabanas the most. They provide a "home base" for family meetups and plenty of space—the Family Suite cabanas hold up to 16 people!

Padded Lounger – Rent two premium loungers with a built-in locker for your belongings. The loungers also have covers for your face. At $29.99 per day (plus tax), this is a great deal, especially since you won't have to pay extra for a locker!

Single Cabana – A private, shaded lounge area for up to 6 people. Starts at $159.99 per day, plus tax.

Family Suite Cabanas – Made for up to 16 people in a spacious cabana area. Prices start at $299.99 per day, plus tax (though most days these will be $599.99 per party, plus tax).

THEMED AREAS

Volcano Bay is broken up into four themed areas. These aren't as drastic in theme as the "dry" parks like Universal Studios and Islands of Adventure. However, they each serve their purpose to deliver thrills or fun splashes for the kids.

Wave Village – Hit the waves or relax on the sand in this seaside simulated beach.

Krakatau – Located inside of the volcano with thrilling slides.

River Village – Sail along on a raft though a lazy river or have fun with your kids in a reef specially designed for them.

Rainforest Village – A collection of family-friendly and thrilling slides.

> **· Magic Tips ·**
> The easiest way to walk through Volcano Bay is through the volcano in the center. There's a trail that leads to most of the sides, thus making it an easier walk than around its base.

KRAKATAU

ATTRACTIONS

KRAKATAU AQUA COASTER

Description: Slide up and down hills around the active volcano in this popular water slide.

Type: Solo tube slide
Perfect for: Families, Tweens, Teens, Thrill Riders
Review: A unique water slide designed like a roller coaster. Ride with your family or group over hills on a toboggan-like raft. The thrill of this ride can be enjoyable to most.
Height Restriction: 42" minimum (under 48" must ride with adult)

· Magic Tips ·
On busier days, this ride can have extremely long wait times. We recommend riding it first.

KALA AND TA NUI SERPENTINE BODY SLIDES
Description: Plunge down the volcano after a trap door opens beneath you!
Type: Solo tube slide
Perfect for: Thrill Riders
Height Restriction: 48" minimum, 230 lbs. maximum weight
Review: An intense plunge into the core of the volcano. For thrill riders, this is a must. Everyone else might want to stay clear! This is the less intense version of the Ko'okiri Body Plunge.

Note: This ride can be pretty intense! Water can easily go up your nose and your body can rattle in the tube, so be careful.

KO'OKIRI BODY PLUNGE
Description: The dreaded red-colored tube! Stand on a trap door before it opens and sends you plummeting at a 70-degree angle!
Type: Solo tube slide
Perfect for: Thrill Riders
Height Restriction: 48" minimum, 300 lbs. maximum weight
Review: An intense plunge straight into core of the volcano. Certainly the most intense slide in the park! We only recommend the Body Plunge for thrill riders.

Note: *Like the Body Slides, we safely cover our noses on this attraction.*

PUNGA RACERS
Description: Race your friends down the hill on this body slide!
Type: Solo water slide
Perfect for: Kids, Tweens, Teens, Adults, Thrill Riders
Height Restriction: 42" minimum (under 48" must ride with adult)
Review: Punga Racers previously used mats. However, Universal updated this attraction to a body slide.

WAVE VILLAGE

ATTRACTIONS

WATURI BEACH
Description: A wave pool in front of the volcano.
Type: Wave pool
Perfect for: Kids, Tweens, Teens, Adults
Height Restriction: Kids under 48" are required to wear a life vest (these are provided by Volcano Bay)
Review: Wade in this pool until the drums start to bang—then get ready for the rush of waves! We only recommend this attraction for strong swimmers unless they keep in the shallow areas. Kids to teens seem to love Waturi Beach the most.

THE REEF
Description: A calmer wave pool in front of the volcano.
Type: Wave pool
Perfect for: Kids, Adults
Height Restriction: Kids under 48" are required to wear a life vest (these are provided by Volcano Bay)

Review: If the waters of Waturi Beach are too strong, but you like the splash of the waves, head to The Reef and enjoy a calmer experience.

RIVER VILLAGE

ATTRACTIONS

KOPIKO WAI WINDING RIVER

Description: A lazy river that winds throughout Volcano Bay.
Type: Lazy river
Perfect for: Kids, Tweens, Teens, Adults
Height Restriction: None
Review: A gentle stream through caves and open air around the water park. Even better if you grab an inner tube and just let the current take you!

> **· Magic Tips ·**
> Look for TapTu Play zones around the lazy river. Here you can scan your TapuTapu bracelet and shoot water cannons or spray at the people in the river!

HONU IKA MOANA

Description: Board a round raft and surf the waves on this massive tube.
Type: Group raft water slide
Perfect for: Kids, Tweens, Teens, Adults, Thrill Riders
Height Restriction: 42" minimum (under 48" must ride with adult)
Review: Based on a legend of islanders who rode whales and sea turtles in the Pacific, you'll cruise over giant crested waves on these thrilling water raft rides.

ATTRACTIONS FOR KIDS

TOT TIKI REEF* – A collection of slides and splash zones designed for young kids.

RUNAMUKKA REEF* – An outdoor water play fortress.

**These areas are designed for Kids under 48"*

RAINFOREST VILLAGE

ATTRACTIONS

MAKU PUIHI ROUND RAFT RIDES

Description: Travel down one of two large waterslides on an inflatable tube.
Type: Group raft water slides
Perfect for: Kids, Tweens, Teens, Adults, Thrill Riders
Height Restriction: 42" minimum (under 48" must ride with adult)
Review: Large water slides with giant rafts big enough to hold a group of six!

TANIWHA TUBES

Description: Ride singles or doubles in this tube slide.
Type: Raft water slides
Perfect for: Kids, Tweens, Teens, Adults, Thrill Riders
Height Restriction: 42" minimum (under 48" must ride with adult)
Review: Located at the edge of Volcano Bay, these fun tube slides typically have short wait times.

OHYA AND OHNO DROP SLIDES

Description: Fast water slides with a plunge.
Type: Solo water slides
Perfect for: Kids, Tweens, Teens, Adults, Thrill Riders
Height Restriction: 48" minimum
Review: Slip, slide, and plunge out of these high-speed water slides designed for single riders without rafts.

TEWAWA THE FEARLESS RIVER

A faster version of the lazy river perfect for floating on a tube. Must be 42" to enter. Kids under 48" are required to wear a life vest (these are provided by Volcano Bay).

PUKA ULI LAGOON

A large pool with splashing water jets designed for relaxing.

CHAPTER EIGHT

HOTEL GUIDE

INTRODUCTION

The Universal Orlando Resort has several uniquely stylized hotels within its property. Whether you're looking for an inexpensive, but great place to stay with your family or something a bit high-end and relaxing, at least one of these hotels is a great fit. Expect friendly staff, clean rooms, and beautiful pools in every location.

HOTEL CLASSIFICATIONS

Premier Hotel – Luxury. These hotels are closest in proximity to the theme parks, CityWalk and amenities.

Preferred Hotel – Deluxe. A bit further away, but water taxis and shuttle buses get you there for free.

Prime Value Hotel – Affordable. Not very close to the parks, but still a great value with free shuttles to the attractions and CityWalk. These are often close to Volcano Bay.

AMENITIES

All Universal Orlando Resort hotels come with the following perks for their guests:

Early Park Admission

Beat the crowds and enter the parks an hour before regular opening times. You'll need a paid admission for entry.

Transportation

Get free transport to CityWalk and the theme parks via water taxi or shuttle. You just need one room key for you and your party to ride. These transports run every 15-20 minutes. The water taxis are the best (and most fun) way to travel throughout the Resort. Hop aboard one of these boats to see lush surroundings—and the skippers are great at answering questions about your visit. No need to tip the captain, but you can if you'd like. The shuttle system is a network of busses that run from hotels to the entrance of the park by the normal roads. You won't get in as close as the water taxis, which drop off in front of the parks and CityWalk, but the busses are completely free to guests.

Room Key Charging

You can add your credit card to your room key for easy charging. Just ask the front desk when you check in for this option. Or add your credit card to your room key via the Universal Orlando application. Much better than carrying around loads of plastic cards!

Free Merchandise Delivery

If you see something you'd like to buy in CityWalk or one of the parks, you don't have to carry it around with you all day. Before purchasing, ask a sales clerk if the item is available for room delivery. Most of the shops within the theme parks and CityWalk have this option.

Exclusive Character Appearances

See your favorite Universal characters up-close and exclusively available to Resort hotel guests. Ask your hotel concierge for details on appearances, as the locations and characters may change.

Golf Universal Orlando
A free shuttle to the Grand Cypress Golf Club in Orlando, about 15 minutes southwest of the Resort (closer to Disney World). These full, green courses come with complimentary clubs and golf balls to use.

> **· Magic Tips ·**
> Universal Orlando often allows pool hopping between its resorts. If you're staying at the Hard Rock Hotel, Portofino Bay, Royal Pacific, Sapphire Falls, Aventura, or Cabana Bay, you're usually allowed to visit other pools on property. However, the Endless Summer resort hotels can only pool hop between themselves.

MORE AMENITIES

Guests of the Hard Rock Hotel, Loews Portofino Bay Hotel, and Loews Royal Pacific Resort can enjoy the following:

Free Universal Express Unlimited
One of the better reasons to pay top dollar for these hotels, Express Unlimited allows you to skip the lines to nearly every attraction in both parks. You'll still need to purchase a park ticket for admission to use Express Unlimited.

Priority Restaurant Seating
Many guests don't use this feature, but you should! If you didn't get a restaurant reservation, make sure to tell the host/hostess that you are staying at one of these three hotels, and the host will move your place earlier.

HOTEL PARKING

- **Hard Rock Hotel, Portofino Bay, & Royal Pacific** – $28 for self-parking, $37 for valet
- **Sapphire Falls** – $26 for self-parking, $45 for valet
- **Cabana Bay and Aventura** – $18 for self-parking
- **Endless Summer** – $15 for self-parking

HARD ROCK HOTEL

5800 Universal Blvd, Orlando, FL 32819 / (407) 503-2000
Best for: Everyone
Theme: Rock and roll in a California mission oasis
Cost: $$$–$$$$
Location: 5-minute walking distance to parks and CityWalk
Review: The Hard Rock is our favorite hotel in the parks for its location, friendly staff, stylized and comfortable rooms, large pool area, and superb dining. Rock 'n' roll memorabilia garnish the lobby and some of the rooms. Outside, look for palms, green grass, and a fountain with guitars near the entrance. Guests of this hotel have access to all amenities including free Universal Express Unlimited and priority restaurant seating. Walking distance to CityWalk's nightlife and the fun of the parks, the hotel is closer to the Universal Studios side than Islands of Adventure. Though Hard Rock is usually the most expensive hotel at Universal—and often sells out during busy months—you can get a discount by booking as early as possible.

ROOMS & SUITES

Every room in the Hard Rock is well-decorated and stylish. You'll often have a choice between a king or two queen beds. Rooms usually have an option for a rollaway bed.

Standard Rooms – 375 sq. ft., sleeps up to 5 guests. Views are often without much scenery, like a parking lot or rooftop.

Garden View Room – 375 sq. ft., sleeps up to 5 guests. Views are of the green, tropical garden.

Pool Room – 375 sq. ft., sleeps up to 5 guests. Your room will look out to the pool. We recommend this view as Hard Rock's pool is stunning.

Deluxe King Rooms – 400 sq. ft., sleeps up to 3 guests. These rooms also come with a sitting area for lounging.

Deluxe Queen Rooms – 500 sq. ft., sleeps up to 5 guests. If you are hosting a larger party, go with this room so that you'll have more space to stretch out than a standard queen room.

Kids Suites – 800 sq. ft. and sleeps up to 5 guests. If you are looking for more space for your family, this a great option. There is a king bed for parents in one room and twin beds for kids in the next. The kids room also comes with smaller-sized furniture for them. Overall, we don't feel these rooms are as well decorated as others, but they are very practical.

King Suites – 650 sq. ft. and sleeps up to 3 guests. The King bed is on one half and the connecting "entertainment room" with sofa and television, is on the other. You can connect up to 3 rooms, including 2 King Suites, to sleep up to 13 guests. All of these suites come with a garden or pool view, depending on your choice.

Hospitality Suites – 1,250 sq. ft. space designed for entertaining guests. Equipped with a full kitchen and dining area, these aren't rooms so much for sleeping as they are for meetings. However, the Hospitality Suite does sleep up to 4 guests with a king bed and a rollaway bed. Unfortunately, there aren't hospitality suites with two queen beds.

Graceland Suite – 2,000 sq. ft. and sleeps 2. If you're looking to impress, the Graceland Suite is the best room on the Resort. It houses large televisions, a lounge, fire place, marble shower, whirlpool tub, walk-in closet, and even a baby grand piano. Celebrities often stay in this suite so the lavishness is meant to meet top standards. We think the Graceland Suite is awesome if you're okay with spending top dollar, but for large parties, book connecting rooms instead, as this space is just meant for a couple.

Club – Access to an exclusive area with water, snacks, breakfast bites, beer, wine, and sometimes vodka mixers for adults 21 and older. The club rooms are located on a higher level and range from standard rooms without views to suites with gorgeous views. You can also request a 2-bedroom on the club level, which would be a king suite attached to a room with two queen beds.

AMENITIES

Pool – Kids and adults love Hard Rock's pool! Designed like a desert oasis, this massive pool has several hot tubs, a water slide, and even a beach-like area. At night, watch kid-friendly movies and order dining from the Beachclub bar. Hard Rock's pool is fairly shallow and mostly for wading, which is ideal for families and adults just looking to cool off. Of course, no pool oasis is complete without numerous lounge chairs and wait service, which Hard Rock perfectly delivers.

Body Rock Fitness Center – Get a workout at this hotel's complimentary gym. Equipped with treadmills, bicycles, ellipticals, free weights, and a stairmaster, the room isn't enormous, but it gets the job done for a vacation pump. The fitness center also maps out jogging paths up to 3 miles around the property and houses a locker room with saunas.

Business Center – Print, copy, fax, mail, and e-mail from this all-in-one self-service room. The business center is open 24 hours, 7 days a week, and is very helpful. Some of the items may cost to use, see concierge desk for details.

Mandara Spa – Located in the Loews Portofino Bay Hotel, this spa isn't very close to the Hard Rock, but it is relaxing. Prepare to spend $150 or more on a massage, though it does offer a set of other services from skincare to body treatments.

MORE AMENITIES

1. Complimentary Wi-Fi
2. Text line for room requests
3. All rooms are non-smoking
4. In-room safe
5. Mini fridge
6. Coffeemaker
7. iHome docking station
8. Turndown service is available upon request of housekeeping
9. Free newspaper upon request
10. If you need a microwave, one can be supplied to your room for a small fee

· Magic Tips ·
Depending on your room location, we have noticed slow speeds with Wi-Fi. In the club rooms, we had better access than further outside room. Yet another reason to request a closer room to the accommodations.

Staying with Pets

The Hard Rock offers pet stays for additional fees, starting at $50 per night and a maximum of $150 for the stay. If you have a dog that is potty trained and doesn't need a lot of exercise, the Hard Rock could be perfect for your needs. There is a small outdoor area for your pet to relieve itself and even room service treat options for dogs. However, if you have a dog with more exercise needs, this may not be the best choice, as Hard Rock is a bit strict and dogs are expected to stay in the room.

Velvet Sessions

See rock and roll legends in this intimate venue. These events happen about once a month and we recommend getting tickets in advance in case the show sells out. Check out the show schedule:
www.hardrockhotelorlando.com/velvet-sessions.htm

· Magic Tips ·

Before leaving the hotel after your stay, head to the front desk to have your room key turned into a complimentary guitar pick!

LOEWS PORTOFINO BAY

5601 Universal Blvd, Orlando, FL 32819 / (407) 503-1000
Best for: Adults, Teens, and Conference Groups
Theme: Italian Resort
Cost: $$$–$$$$
Location: 15-minute walking distance to parks and CityWalk, 10-minute water taxi ride
Review: Portofino Bay has a European charm unlike anywhere else in Orlando. If you are looking for a quieter hotel, Portofino Bay is a great choice. This luxury hotel offers stunning views, delicious dining, and premium rooms. At night, the hotel's waterfront plaza comes to life with guests strolling to the many dining locations. Though you can walk to the parks and CityWalk, it's just a quick water taxi ride to the entrances. Overall, we enjoy the Portofino Bay for its amenities and proximity to the parks. Though Hard Rock is much closer and has the superior pool, Loews houses some fine eateries, charm, and décor that leave a great impression.

Note: Portofino Bay tends to house conferences throughout the year. At these times, the place can become packed and availability may be low. To avoid this, book as far in advance as possible.

ROOMS & SUITES

The rooms at Portofino Bay have a European feel with the molding accents, clean white bedding, and door styles. The bathrooms are often spacey and the beds are comfortable.

Garden View Rooms – 450 sq. ft., sleeps up to 5 guests and comes with either a king or 2 queen beds. Views are of the green, tropical garden.

Bay View Rooms – 450 sq. ft., sleeps up to 5 guests. Your room will look out to the water. We recommend this room for the best views.

Deluxe Rooms – 490 sq. ft., sleeps up to 3 guests with a king or 2 queens. They also come with a sitting area for lounging and an expansive bathroom.

Deluxe King or 2 Queen Rooms – 490 sq. ft., sleeps up to 5 guests. Our favorite room for the price. These rooms are spacious and have an Italian window that connects to the bathroom. Also available on the club level for extra amenities.

Portofino Parlor Suites with Connecting Room – Starting at 450 sq. ft. Get a bonus space for a rollaway bed and sleep up to 7. The connecting room can be a King or 2 Queen with bay or garden view. Rollaway beds are $25 per night.

Hospitality Parlor Suites with Connecting Room – 920 sq. ft. with space for up to 5. This suite is designed for entertaining guests and includes sofas, armchairs, a kitchenette with fridge and microwave, and two bathrooms with the connecting room. You can attach a King or 2 Queen Garden View room.

Despicable Me Kids' Suites – 650 sq. ft., and up to 4 guests. The Minions from *Despicable Me* take over this colorful, kid-friendly room. With specially designed twin beds, curtains, wallpaper and more, this suite attaches to a king room for adults. Additional rollaway or crib upon request with $25/ rollaway bed.

Villa Parlor Suite with Connecting Room – 1600 sq. ft. and sleeps 10. The largest room with a connecting bay view or garden view suite. There are two separate bedrooms and a large living room area. Rollaway beds are available for $25 per night.

Club – Access to an exclusive area with water, snacks, breakfast bites, beer, wine, and sometimes vodka mixers for adults 21 and older. Unfortunately, the club level guest rooms are pretty far away from the club amenities, so you'll need to walk a bit before getting to the area. The club room is open from 7am to 10pm daily.

AMENITIES

Pools – Like right out of a Roman aqueduct are blue waters and brick walls. Wade in the water, race down the waterslide, or lounge on the beach chairs. The Hillside Pool is more for adults, offering a calm swimming experience with little noise.

Mandara Spa Fitness Center – Get in a complimentary workout at this hotel's gym. Equipped with treadmills, bicycles, ellipticals, weight resistance machines, free weights, a stairmaster, and fitness mats. The room isn't enormous, but it gets the job done for a vacation pump. The fitness center also maps out jogging paths up to 3 miles around the property and houses a locker room with saunas.

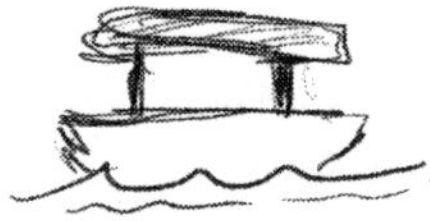

Business Center – Print, copy, fax, mail, and e-mail from this all-in-one self-service room. The business center is open 24 hours, 7 days a week, and is very helpful. Some of the items may cost to use, see concierge desk for details.

Mandara Spa – A beautiful and relaxing spa experience. Prepare to spend $150 or more on a massage, though it does offer a set of other services from skincare to body treatments.

Kids' Gifts – For children under 10, Portofino Bay offers a complimentary welcome gift of assorted items for young kids. A "Kids Closet" is also available to borrow with toys, books, a night light, blankets, outlet protectors, and more to make your stay with children more comfortable. Babysitting services are also offered with the concierge. For older kids, board games and an on-site arcade are offered to play.

MORE AMENITIES

1. Complimentary Wi-Fi
2. All rooms are non-smoking
3. In-room safe
4. Mini fridge
5. Coffeemaker
6. iHome docking station
7. Turndown service is available upon request
8. Free newspaper upon request
9. If you need a microwave, one can be supplied to your room for a small fee
10. Dry cleaning is available Monday through Saturday, same day, for an additional fee.

Staying with Pets

Portofino Bay offers pet stays for additional fees, starting at $50 per night and a maximum of $150 for the stay. Portofino Bay brags to be one of the better resorts to stay at with pets, as part of Loews hospitality experience. Potty areas and walking spots are available around the Resort. Still, we recommend a very well-potty-trained dog that is okay staying in a room for most of the day.

LOEWS ROYAL PACIFIC

6300 Hollywood Way, Orlando, FL 32819 / (407) 503-3000
Best for: Families, Adults
Theme: Polynesian Resort
Cost: $$$
Location: 10-minute walking distance to parks and CityWalk, 10-minute water taxi ride
Review: Third in line for luxury and proximity to the parks, Royal Pacific feels like a Polynesian paradise centered around a lagoon-style pool. The rooms aren't as pricey as Hard Rock or Portofino Bay, but you get the same benefits including Express Pass Unlimited. Depending on availability, Royal Pacific can be more expensive than Portofino Bay, but this occurrence is quite rare.

ROOMS & SUITES

The rooms at Royal Pacific are undeniably stylish with tropical flares, artwork, and contemporary-style bedding. While these rooms tend to run smaller than the ones at Portofino Bay and Hard Rock, the kids' rooms and hospitality parlors are much larger.

Standard Rooms – 335 sq. ft., sleeps up to 5 guests and comes with either a king or 2 queen beds. Views are of the garden, tropical garden. They also have a desk and chair for office work.

Water View Rooms – Same as the standard rooms, but with a view of the pool or the water way. We prefer the views of the beautiful water way to watch the boats come and go.

Deluxe Rooms – 490 sq. ft., sleeps up to 3 guests with a king or 2 queens. They also come with a sitting area for lounging and an expansive bathroom.

Deluxe King or 2 Queen Rooms – 490 sq. ft., sleeps up to 5 guests. Our favorite room for the price and the deal. These rooms are fairly spacious. Also available on the club level for extra amenities.

Hospitality Parlor Suite with Connecting Room – 1,005 sq. ft. with space for up to 5. This suite is designed for entertaining guests and includes sofas, armchairs, a kitchenette with fridge and microwave, and two bathrooms with the connecting room. You can attach a King or 2 Queen Garden View room.

Jurassic World Kids' Suites – 670 sq. feet and up to 5 guests. This jungle and dinosaur-themed room brings the fun of *Jurassic World* to a kid-sized space. With specially designed twin beds, curtains, wallpaper and more, this suite attaches to a King bed master bedroom. Additional rollaway or crib upon request with $25/rollaway bed.

Royal Club Rooms – These 335 sq. ft. rooms are either a King or a Queen suite with varying views of the water way, pool, or garden. Access to an exclusive area with water, snacks, breakfast bites, beer, wine, dessert, and sometimes vodka mixers for adults 21 and older. The club room is open from 7am to 9.30pm daily.

AMENITIES

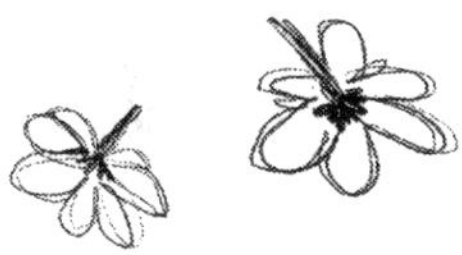

Pools – This massive and gorgeous pool is surrounded by cabanas, two hot tubs, and even a water play area for kids. Nearly every night there are activities at the pool from hula hoop contests to nightly movies. Cabanas are available for rental at an additional cost, but the rest comes with your reservation.

Mandara Spa – Located in the Loews Portofino Bay Hotel, the location isn't very close, but the spa is relaxing. Prepare to spend $150 or more on a massage, though it does offer a set of other services from skincare to body treatments. The best way to get to Portofino Bay from Royal Pacific is by the free water taxi.

Business Center – Print, copy, fax, mail, and e-mail from this all-in-one self-service room. The business center is open 24 hours, 7 days a week, and is very helpful. Some of the services may have a fee—see concierge desk for details.

Gym – A large 5,000+ sq. ft. exercise room with weights, strength training machines, exercise bikes, stairmaster, ellipticals, a steam room, sauna, and maps to jogging and walking paths up to 3 miles in length.

MORE AMENITIES

1. Complimentary Wi-Fi
2. All rooms are non-smoking
3. In-room safe
4. Mini fridge
5. Coffeemaker
6. iHome docking station
7. Turndown service is available upon request of housekeeping
8. Free newspaper upon request
9. If you need a microwave, one can be supplied to your room for a small fee
10. Dry cleaning is available Monday through Saturday, same day, for an additional fee.

Staying with Pets

Royal Pacific offers pet stays for additional fees, starting at $50 per night and a maximum of $150 for the stay. Loews brags to be one of the better resorts to stay at with pets, as part of their hospitality. Potty areas and walking spots are available around the Resort. Still, we recommend a very well-potty-trained dog that is okay staying in a room for most of the day.

ENTERTAINMENT

WANTILAN LUAU AT THE WANTILAN PAVILION
See hula dancers and fire spinners while you dine at this buffet show. The luau is usually on Friday nights and the buffet is all-you-can eat and includes sodas, tea, water, wine, beer, and Mai Tais (alcohol for those 21 and older). The Polynesian-inspired food is great and so is the show!

PRICES
Adults: $71-$91
Children 3-9: $36-$51
Children under 3: No cost
Reservations highly recommended. The higher priced seating has better views of the stage and dancers. Higher tiers also receive a complimentary souvenir tiki mug to take home!

SHOPPING

Toko Gifts – A small convenience store with snacks, sunscreen, pain killers, toiletries, drinks, and some apparel.

Treasures of Bali – An apparel store with resort-style clothing, swim suits, and even grass skirts. This store also sells Universal Orlando gifts and souvenirs.

LOEWS SAPPHIRE FALLS

6601 Adventure Way, Orlando, FL 32819 / (407) 503-5000
Best for: Families, Adults
Theme: Modern and Tropical Resort
Cost: $$$
Location: 10-minute water taxi ride, ½ mile walk to the Parks
Review: A resort hotel with stunning creeks, a large pool, trendy restaurants, and beautiful rooms. Located near Volcano Bay, and between Cabana Bay and Royal Pacific, the hotel

aims to please guests looking for an upscale resort hotel without the high cost.

ROOMS & SUITES

These fresh, newly designed rooms are modern, tropical styles. The rooms are even smaller than Royal Pacific, but the design is similar. We like the overall clean layout of these rooms and they're great for the price.

Standard – 321 sq. ft., sleeps up to 5 guests and come with either a king or 2 queen beds. Views are of the garden, tropical garden. They also have a desk and chair for office work.

Pool View Room – Same as the standard rooms, but with a view of the pool.

Lagoon View Room – Same as the standard rooms, but with a view of the water.

King Suite – 529 sq. ft., sleeps up to 3 guests. They also come with a sitting area for lounging and an expansive bathroom.

Hospitality Suite – 1353 sq. ft. with space for up to 5. This suite is designed for entertaining guests and includes sofas, a kitchenette with fridge and microwave, and a spacious bathroom.

Kids' Suites – 529 sq. feet and up to 5 guests. These attached rooms only allow access to the main hall view the via parent room. With specially designed twin beds, curtains, wallpaper and more, it attaches to a king bed master bedroom. Additional rollaway or crib upon request with $25/ rollaway bed.

Sapphire Suite – 851 sq. ft., sleeps up to 5 guests. These large rooms are beautifully designed with a wet bar and large bathrooms. Unfortunately, the room only comes with a king bed, though rollaway beds are possible with advanced notice.

AMENITIES

Pools – A large, lagoon-style lagoon is the centerpiece of this resort. There are plenty of lounge chairs, a large hot tub, and even a water slide.

Mandara Spa – Located a bit further away in the Loews Portofino Bay Hotel. It's worth a trip to this soothing, high-end spa. Prepare to spend $150 or more on a massage, though it does offer a set of other services from skincare to body treatments. The best way to get to Portofino Bay from Sapphire Falls is by water taxi.

Kaline Health and Fitness – A spacious gym with a dry sauna, new weightlifting equipment, ellipticals, and treadmills.

MORE AMENITIES

1. Complimentary Wi-Fi
2. All rooms are non-smoking
3. In-room safe
4. Mini fridge
5. Turndown service is available upon request of housekeeping

Staying with Pets

Sapphire Falls offers pet stays for additional fees, starting at $50 per night and a maximum of $150 for the stay. Loews brags to be one of the better resorts to stay at with pets, as part of their hospitality. Potty areas and walking spots are available around the Resort. Still, we recommend a very well-potty-trained dog that is okay staying in a room for most of the day.

SHOPPING

The Universal Store – Apparel, accessories, and toys inspired by the characters and attractions at Universal Studios and Islands of Adventure.

CABANA BAY

6550 Adventure Way, Orlando, FL 32819 / (407) 503-4000
Best for: Families, Adults
Theme: Swanky Beach Resort
Cost: $$
Location: 15-minute walk or a shuttle
Review: A swanky family-friendly hotel. With the best prices, tons of activities, and a pool with a lazy river, Cabana Bay is often the best choice for families on a budget.

AMENITIES

Pool – A lagoon-style pool with palm trees, lounge chairs, a lazy river for floating, and a waterslide. The second Cabana pool has a beach-like feel with cabanas available for rental.

Free Wi-Fi – Basic internet around the hotel.

Jack LaLanne Physical Fitness Studio – A gym with weightlifting equipment, ellipticals, treadmills, and classic video fitness instruction by Jack LaLanne.

ROOMS & SUITES

The retro décor is straight out of the 60's. Bright colors, cool designs, and even bright orange chairs add a sense of light fun to Cabana Bay. The hotel is set up perfectly for families of all sizes at an affordable cost with many amenities. Being that this is a family resort, there aren't any rooms with just king-sized beds.

Standard Rooms – Sleeps up to 4 guests with 2 queen beds. Views are of the garden, building, or obstructed. They also have a chair and table for crafts.

Poolside Rooms – Same as the standard rooms, but with a view of the pool.

Volcano Side Rooms – Same as the standard rooms, but with a view of Volcano Bay.

Courtyard Family Suites – Sleep up to 6 in this larger room with 2 queen beds, a large bathroom with his/her sinks, a kitchenette, and a pull-out sofa. These rooms come with various views, including poolside, and are either in the main building or the tower.

2-Bedroom Suites – A 772-sq ft. room with two baths, three beds, and a pull-out sofa. One room has two full beds and the second smaller room has one queen bed.

Staying with Pets – Pets are not allowed.

ENTERTAINMENT

Game-O-Rama Arcade – Filled with games from current to old school.

Galaxy Bowl – A 10-lane bowling alley with an attached restaurant. Cost is $15 per game for adults and $9 per kid under 12. Games last 60-90 minutes. Hotel parking fees charged for visiting guests with cars.

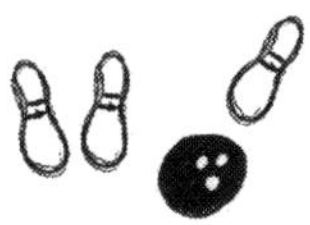

SHOPPING

The Universal Store – Apparel, accessories, and toys inspired by the characters and attractions at Universal Studios and Islands of Adventure.

AVENTURA HOTEL

6725 Adventure Way, Orlando, FL 32819 / (407) 503-6000
Best for: Young Adults, Adults
Theme: Modern and Stylish Hotel Tower
Cost: $$
Location: 15-minute walk or a shuttle, 5 minutes to Volcano Bay
Review: Universal's Aventura Hotel is located just steps away from Universal's Volcano Bay water park. The tower-style is modern, sleek, and filled with new technology such as tablets for ordering fresh towels, room service, and even for playing Netflix. The rooms have curved structures and offer sweeping views of the city including the Orlando Eye Ferris Wheel in the distance. The rooftop bar is also set to appeal to young adults. With comfort and style at a great price, Aventura is an upscale getaway for those on a budget.

AMENITIES

Pool – A large, sleek pool at the base of the hotel. It offers a kids' splash zone and a fire pit.

Free Wi-Fi – Basic internet around the hotel.

Fitness Center – A gym with weightlifting equipment, ellipticals, and treadmills.

Game Room – New arcade games and Virtual Reality!

ROOMS & SUITES

Bright and clean rooms designed to bring some relaxation to your stay. The hotel is smoke-free.

Standard 2 Queen Room – 314 square feet. Sleeps up to 4 guests with 2 queen beds.

Standard King Room – 258 square feet. Sleeps up to 4 guests with 1 king bed and a pull-out bed.

Deluxe 2 Queen– 385 square feet. Sleeps up to 5 guests with 2 queen beds.

Deluxe King Room – 385 square feet. Sleeps up to 4 guests with 1 king bed and a pull-out bed.

Skyline View 2 Queen Room – 314 square feet. Sleeps up to 4 guests with 2 queen beds, and has a sweeping view of Orlando or the Universal Resort.

Staying with Pets – Pets are not allowed at this hotel.

SHOPPING

The Universal Store – Apparel, accessories, and toys inspired by the characters and attractions at Universal Studios and Islands of Adventure.

SURFSIDE INN

7000 Universal Blvd, Orlando, FL 32819 / (407) 503-7000
Best for: Families on a budget, Young Adults
Theme: California-style beach hotel
Cost: $
Location: 5-10 minute shuttle to the Universal theme parks
Review: Part of the Endless Summer Resort, Universal's concept for a California-style beach inn provides very

affordable accommodations. The rooms have a breezy, simple feel and the beds are reasonably comfortable. The style is beach house with balsa wood, indoor picnic tables, and wood-like flooring. There are also plenty of in-room power outlets for device charging, free shuttles to the Universal theme parks, and early access to the parks on select dates. Best of all, families needing more space will find 2-bedroom suites starting around $130 a night! This unheard of price makes it the best value for staying within the Resort.

AMENITIES

Pool – A large, surfboard-shaped pool with activities such as giant board games and other fun occurring daily.

Free Wi-Fi – Basic internet around the hotel.

Fitness Center – A gym with new weightlifting equipment, ellipticals, and treadmills.

Game Room – New arcade games (at an additional price).

ROOMS & SUITES

Rooms start at an unbelievable $85 a night for a standard room and $131 for a 2-bedroom suite! These prices are often available when bundled for multiple-night stays and do not include tax. All rooms come with a TV, mini fridge, in-room safe, ironing board (with iron), telephone, outlets (including USB outlets), alarm clock, and hairdryer. 2-bedroom suites are technically more like a 1-bedroom, with the main room having two queen beds and a kitchenette with microwave, and the second room having an additional TV and an additional queen bed.

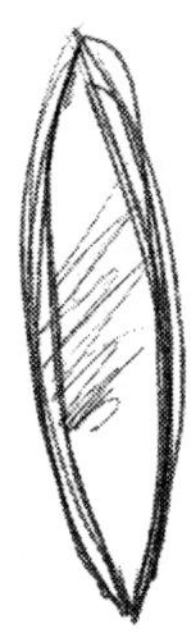

Standard Room – 313 square feet. Sleeps up to 4 guests with 2 queen beds, one bath, and a single sink with vanity. Option of standard or pool view.

2-Bedroom Suite – 440 square feet. Sleeps up to 6 guests with 3 queen beds, one bath, in-room picnic table, and a dual sink with vanity. Options with standard, pool, or lake view.

Staying with Pets – Pets are not allowed at this hotel.

SHOPPING

The Universal Store – Apparel, accessories, and toys inspired by Universal them park attractions.

DOCKSIDE INN

7125 Universal Blvd, Orlando, FL 32819 / (888) 273-1311
Best for: Families on a budget, Young Adults
Theme: California-style beach hotel
Cost: $
Location: 5-10 minute shuttle to the Universal theme parks
Review: Part of the Endless Summer Resort, the Dockside Inn and Suites is very similar to its sister hotel, the Surfside Inn and Suites. The rooms are standard or 2-bedroom suites with plenty of beds for all visitors. The layouts and pricing in both resorts are nearly identical. However, Dockside offers two pools and more rooms than Surfside.

AMENITIES

Pool – Two pools at the center of each building.

Free Wi-Fi – Basic internet around the hotel.

Fitness Center – A gym with new weightlifting equipment, ellipticals, and treadmills.

Game Room – New arcade games (at an additional price).

ROOMS & SUITES

Standard Room – 313 square feet. Sleeps up to 4 guests with 2 queen beds, one bath, and a single sink with vanity. Option of standard or pool view.

2-Bedroom Suite – 440 square feet. Sleeps up to 6 guests with 3 queen beds, one bath, in-room picnic table, and a dual sink with vanity. Option of standard, pool, or water view.

Staying with Pets – Pets are not allowed at this hotel.

· **Magic Tips** ·
Though Universal's Surfside and Dockside Inns are further away from the theme parks than its other hotels, traffic patterns have allowed shuttles from the Endless Summer area to transport guests faster than Cabana Bay!

SHOPPING

The Universal Store – Apparel, accessories, and toys inspired by the characters and attractions at Universal Studios and Islands of Adventure.

TOP OFF-SITE HOTELS

While staying at a Universal Orlando hotel has its benefits from early park access to complimentary shuttles, you may be able to find even more amenities at a lower price with a nearby Orlando hotel. We've compiled a list of our top choice hotels outside of the Universal Orlando Resort.

ROSEN SHINGLE CREEK ORLANDO

9939 Universal Blvd, Orlando, FL 32819
(866) 996-6338 / www.rosenshinglecreek.com
Distance from Universal: About 4 miles
Cost: $$ **Star Rating:** 4
Review: Our favorite off-site hotel is the Rosen Shingle Creek. This stunning property is just outside of the Universal Orlando Resort and placed on an award-winning golf course. The staff is friendly, the rooms are beautiful and comfortable, and if you book ahead, you can get a very good deal on a room.
Amenities: Several pools (family, quiet, and kids' wading pool), hot tubs, tennis courts, walking trails, game room, basketball court, volleyball court, fishing (seasonal). Stay at the hotel and receive 25% off of golfing green fees (first round only). Shuttle to Universal is available with reservation: +1 (407) 996-8596
Discounts: The Rosen Shingle Creek offers several theme park vacation packages including tickets to Universal Orlando. For their select packages, visit the hotel's website: **https://www.rosenshinglecreek.com/specials/leisure-packages**

THE POINT HOTEL & SUITES

7389 Universal Blvd, Orlando, FL 32819
(407) 956-2000 / www.thepointorlando.com
Distance from Universal: About 1.5 miles
Cost: $-$$

Review: A popular hotel for its proximity to the Universal Orlando Resort, the Point Hotel and Suites offer spacious rooms for a great price. Guests also enjoy the shuttle service to and from the theme parks and airport.
Amenities: Shuttle service to Orlando hotspots (Universal Orlando, Disney, Sea World, and the Orlando International Airport), gym, concierge, business center, Wi-Fi, pool, hot tub
Discounts: Get seasonal discounts and take advantage of promotions for booking early:
https://www.thepointorlando.com/offers.htm

· **Magic Tips** ·
Typically the best rates for off-site hotels are found on third-party websites (ie: Priceline.com, Expedia, and Orbitz). However, be careful in choosing a reputable source for your booking.

MORE OFF-SITE HOTELS

Hyatt Regency Grand Cypress
1 Grand Cypress Blvd, Orlando, FL 32836
(407) 239-1234 / www.hyatt.com

Star Rating	Our Rating	Price	Shuttle to Universal	Pool
4	A	Deluxe	Yes	Yes

Pros: Beautiful property and rooms. Scheduled shuttle service to and from Universal and Disney theme parks, on-site spa, nearby golfing, rock climbing, and 24-hour fitness center. Pet accommodations available.
Cons: Can be expensive and have a very high resort fee (about $40/night). About a 15-minute drive to the Universal Orlando Resort.

Doubletree by Hilton at the Entrance to Universal Orlando
14200 Bonnet Creek Resort Ln, Orlando, FL 32821
(407) 597-5500 / doubletree3.hilton.com/en/index.html

Star Rating	Our Rating	Price	Shuttle to Universal	Pool
5	A+	Luxury	Yes	Yes

Pros: An affordable 4-star hotel property very close to Universal (less than a 5-minute drive). Hilton Honors members can get discounts on rooms and earn points.
Cons: Rooms are a bit dated. Shuttle service to other theme parks must be scheduled 24 hours in advance.

Gaylord Palms Resort
6000 W. Osceola Parkway, Orlando, FL 32821
(407) 586-0000 / www.gaylordpalms.com

Star Rating	Our Rating	Price	Shuttle to Universal	Pool
5	A-	Luxury	Paid	Yes

Pros: Beautiful and affordable 4-star hotel property and rooms. Unique theming including an indoor restaurant on a boat. Shuttle service to Disney theme parks, on-site spa, pools with waterslides, wave pool, on-site alligators, nearby golfing, and 24-hour fitness center. Marriott Rewards members can get discounts on rooms and earn points. 10-minute drive to Epcot.
Cons: Shuttles to Universal are $21/person roundtrip (thus, we recommend taking Uber or Lyft). Parking is expensive and can become backed up on busy weekends and holidays. The hotel is about a 25-minute drive to Universal Orlando.

Ritz-Carlton Grande Lakes
4012 Central Florida Pkwy, Orlando, FL 32837
(407) 206-2400 / www.ritzcarlton.com

Star Rating	Our Rating	Price	Shuttle to Universal	Pool
5	A	Luxury	Yes	Yes

Pros: Elegant 5-star hotel property and stunning rooms. Shuttle service to and from Universal Orlando, Disney theme parks, and SeaWorld. On-site spa, butterfly garden, kids play area, bocce ball courts, 18-hole golfing, and fitness center. Superior service.
Cons: Expensive, so if you're looking for a bargain on a 5-star resort, you may want to try the Waldorf Astoria (though we prefer the Ritz Carlton or the Four Seasons). About a 20- to 25-minute drive to the Magic Kingdom, Epcot, or Universal Orlando.

CHAPTER NINE

UNIVERSAL CITYWALK

INTRODUCTION

The Universal CityWalk is a mall meets entertainment hotspot. Guests do not need theme park admission to enter this shopping district. During the day, CityWalk is home to a collection of shops and chain restaurants like Bubba Gump and the Hard Rock Cafe. At night, the dance clubs light up and locals pour into the area. You can also catch a movie, sing karaoke, or play mini golf.

We love the scenery in CityWalk with its neon lights, elaborately themed restaurants, and the electric nightlife. Overall, CityWalk is a tourist Mecca (or tourist *trap*, whichever way you'd like to think of it). The lively atmosphere feels like a family-friendly Vegas without the casinos. Instead, you'll have plenty of entertainment options and dining choices from which to choose. Even better, CityWalk is just a short walk from both Universal Orlando theme parks.

Note: We detail the CityWalk's restaurants in the next chapter.

ENTERTAINMENT

UNIVERSAL CINEMARK

See a newly released movie or experience the stunning visuals of the new THX XD Theatre. Now enjoy reserved stadium seating with comfortable recliners. The theater also has a full bar. We recommend seeing a movie in their XD theatre which offers a giant screen and surround sound!

· Magic Tips ·

Parking is free with two paid matinee tickets (11am - 6pm) to the Universal Cinemark movie theatre. Parking must be prepaid and will be reimbursed after purchasing tickets.

CITYWALK'S RISING STAR

Take karaoke to the next level with a live band and even backup singers. The audience area is intimate and it's fun to cheer on the performers. Mostly drinks with a few choice beverages. Open daily from 8pm to midnight.

· Magic Tips ·

If you'd like to perform, get there and choose your song by 9pm to get called on stage.

HARD ROCK LIVE

See big name music stars, comedians, and DJs in this colosseum that fits up to 3,000 concerts-goers.
For the event calendar and tickets:
www.hardrock.com/live/locations/orlando/calendar.aspx

HOLLYWOOD DRIVE-IN GOLF
Play miniature golf in the horror or sci-fi movies! This colorful and creative course has fun for all ages. Choose from The Haunting of Ghostly Greens or Invaders from Planet Putt. Open from 9am – midnight. For discount tickets, book in advance: www.hollywooddriveingolf.com

NIGHT CLUBS

RED COCONUT CLUB
A night club and lounge for those 21 and older. The tropical, Miami feel mixes socializing with live DJ music. Drinks are moderately priced.

UNIQUE SHOPS

Hart and Huntington Tattoo Company – An authentic tattoo parlor. Must be 18 or older.

Quiet Flight Surf Shop – Beach clothing and accessories.

Universal Legacy Store – Clothing and gifts inspired by Universal Studios. Get everything from retro memorabilia to Harry Potter merchandise in this unique shop.

CHAPTER TEN

DINING GUIDE

INTRODUCTION

We've searched the Universal Orlando Resort from top to bottom to find the best eats around (we also know which ones to avoid). The gems aren't always the most expensive or the most obvious. Some of these better dining locations deserve a spot on your to-do list. In this chapter, we venture through the Universal Orlando eateries—from the theme park to the hotels and the fun of CityWalk—and help you plan where to dine.

DINING TYPES

Bars and Lounges – Areas with open seating and typically a full bar.

Quick Service – Fast order meals where you often choose your own seating.

Table Service – Restaurants with a waiter. It is suggested that you tip based on the service you receive.

UNIVERSAL DINING PLAN

Universal Orlando offers special dining packages for use around the Resort. The Universal Dining Plan (UDP) is designed for guests to pre-pay for the food that they plan to enjoy during their vacation. While Universal touts its dining plan as a way to save money, for many guests this simply isn't the case. So, think of UDP as more of an "all-inclusive" cost rather than a way to pinch pennies. However, we've discovered that UDP *can* save you a load of cash or end up costing you more, depending on how well you plan before your visit. Overall, we think that UDP can be a great option for visiting guests, and with our tips, you can make the most of this program. UDP can be redeemed at over a hundred dining spots around Universal Orlando that take part of this program. These include the theme parks and CityWalk (we note most of their locations later in this chapter).

· Magic Tips ·
Universal ended its dining plans in 2021. However, we are listing available plans should they return in 2024.

QUALIFICATIONS

To buy one of the Universal Dining Plans, you'll need to pre-purchase a vacation or ticket package through UniversalOrlando.com or over the phone. The Coca-Cola "freestyle" Souvenir Cup can be purchased on your visit date as a refillable drink mug.

Note: The "freestyle" Souvenir Cup and Universal Quick Service dining plans can also be purchased during Halloween Horror Nights.

DINING PLAN TYPES

UNIVERSAL DINING PLAN

(Must purchase with Vacation Package)

Cost: Prices vary depending on number of days staying.

Credits per guest, per day:

- 1 Table Service Meal (*includes 1 entree, 1 dessert, and 1 non-alcoholic beverage per day*)
- 1 Quick Service Meal (*includes 1 entree and 1 non-alcoholic beverage per day*)
- 1 Snack
- 1 Non-Alcoholic Beverage

UNIVERSAL DINING PLAN – QUICK SERVICE

Cost: $25.99/Adult and $17.99/Child (ages 3-9) per day, plus tax

Credits per guest, per day:

- 1 Quick Service Meal
- 1 Snack
- 1 Non-Alcoholic Beverage

UNIVERSAL DINING PLAN – QUICK SERVICE + SOUVENIR CUP

Cost: $34.99/Adult and $26.99/Child (ages 3-9) per day, plus tax

Credits per guest, per day:

- 1 Quick Service Meal
- 1 Snack
- 1-Day Unlimited Coca-Cola "Freestyle" Beverage

COCA-COLA "freestyle" SOUVENIR CUP

Cost: $16.99/day, plus tax

- 1-Day Unlimited Coca-Cola "Freestyle" Beverage

DINING PLAN TIPS

If you're a heavy soda drinker (or are planning on having about 3 or more per day), the Souvenir Cup is a great value, especially when combined with the Quick Service dining plan.

You can also save money if you're willing to try the most expensive items on the menu. For example, a steak dinner would normally cost more than a hamburger, so it's a better value to select the steak.

Dining Plan snacks can be used for cart items including popcorn, ice cream, and, yes—Butterbeer in the Wizarding World of Harry Potter! Butterbeer is one of the more expensive snacks around Universal, so we recommend using your credit for that. Keep in mind that while the UDP works at the Harry Potter Quick Service locations, character dining experiences (like Marvel and Despicable Me) are not included, even as a Table Service credit. Keep in mind that none of the hotels take part in the Universal Dining Plan and gratuity isn't included, so make sure you bring cash with you to tip (Table Service restaurants only).

As we've said before, depending on your needs, the Universal Dining Plan may not save you money. It may even cost you more than just paying out of pocket for your meals. If you're not interested in planning all of your dining before you head to the parks, we don't recommend the UDP. It might feel overwhelming to pre-plan your vacation, meal by meal for each day. However, the Quick Service plan may work better for your needs in this occasion. It almost always works out to a wash or a slight savings. With this plan, you can grab food when you're hungry and not worry about getting the best bang for your buck.

Also, children 10 and older with smaller appetites may end up costing you more than they'll eat. While some ten-year-olds eat as much as an adult, many do not. Nonetheless, you'll pay the same for a 10-year-old boy as you would an adult man. Furthermore, children who are picky and inconsistent eaters may not benefit from UDP. Make sure you review kids' menus before booking.

MOBILE ORDERING

The Universal Orlando mobile app is your ticket to fast and easy ordering to a select few dining locations in the Resort. Simply order your food using the Universal Orlando app and pick up when its ready!

· Magic Tips ·
Universal Orlando may change out which dining spots offer mobile ordering, and the list has frequently changed. We recommend checking out which dining spots have mobile ordering by looking under the menu in the Universal Orlando app.

Using Mobile Ordering:
1. Download the Universal Orlando app
2. Create a login (or log in with your existing account)
3. Tap the Menu Icon (usually 3 lines in the corner)
4. Tap "Mobile Food & Drink Ordering"
5. Choose your destination and select your items
6. Review the order and purchase with credit card
7. You'll be notified when your order is ready!

OUR RESTAURANT PRICING

$ – Under $10 (typically Snack Carts)
$$ – $10 - $20 (typically Quick Service Restaurants)
$$$ – $20 - $40 (Table Service Restaurants)
$$$$ – More than $40 (Fine Dining)

KEYS

Ω – Uses the Universal Dining Plan (though may not be available in 2024)
❤ – Our most-recommended dining spots and dishes

THEME PARK DINING

UNIVERSAL STUDIOS

CAFE LA BAMBA
Hollywood
Description: Meet some of your favorite characters including the Minions from *Despicable Me* while dining on American favorites.
Type: Character Dining Cafeteria
Price: $$
Menu Items: BBQ ribs, steak, roasted chicken, salad, burritos, tacos
Recommendation: Chipotle BBQ Ribs or Chimichurri Skirt Steak

CENTRAL PARK CREPES ❤
Hollywood
Description: A snack cart with sweet and savory crepes.
Type: Quick Service
Price: $
Menu Items: crepes with different toppings, soda
Recommendation: Smoked Brisket (savory crepe), Strawberry Hazelnut (sweet crepe)

MEL'S DRIVE-IN Ω
Hollywood
Description: A classic 50s diner styled after the film *American Graffiti*. We love the theming, but the bland menu could use a revamp.
Type: Quick service
Price: $$
Menu Items: burgers, onion rings, fries, root beer floats, and shakes
Recommendation: The burgers are okay, but the onion rings are a good choice as a side

FAST FOOD BOULEVARD Ω ❤

Springfield

Description: A collection of cafeteria dining spots styled after locations and characters from The Simpsons.

Type: Quick Service

Price: $-$$

Dining Choices:

Cletus' Chicken Shack – fried chicken and milkshakes

Frying Dutchman – fried seafood and milkshakes

Krusty Burger – burgers and shakes

Lisa's Teahouse of Horror – vegetarian options and mixed tea drinks

Luigi's Pizza – pizzas and milkshakes

Recommendation: Chicken and Waffle Sandwich (Cletus' Chicken Shack), Basket of Calamari (Frying Dutchman), or a Krusty Burger (Krusty Burger)

FINNEGAN'S BAR & GRILL Ω

New York

Description: An Irish-American pub. The options here are hit or miss, but the environment is fun. Finnegan's looks like a place on a movie set. The food is also very similar to what is served in the Harry Potter restaurants.

Type: Table Service

Price: $$$

Menu Items: Cornish pasties, Potato and Onion Webb, Scotch eggs, chicken fingers, bangers and mash, shepherd's pie, fish, chicken, sandwiches, burgers, Guinness Beef Stew

Recommendation: Cornish Pasti or Fish and Chips

THE LEAKY CAULDRON Ω ❤

Diagon Alley

Description: Dine like a witch or wizard in this stunningly detailed British restaurant. See artifacts straight from the *Harry Potter* series and savor delicious offerings inspired by the movies and books! The Leaky Cauldron is one of our favorite dining spots in Universal.

Type: Quick Service

Price: $$

Menu Items: fish and chips, bangers and mash, Guinness stew, fisherman's pie, toad in the hole, mini pies, chicken sandwich, *Harry Potter*-themed desserts, Butterbeer
Recommendation: Specialty Chicken Sandwich ❤, Fish & Chips, Butterbeer Potted Cream ❤

LOMBARD'S SEAFOOD GRILLE Ω

San Francisco
Description: San Franciscan seafood diner on the water. With its rustic charm and view of the Universal waterway, you'll feel like you've been transported to an authentic Californian restaurant on the wharf!
Type: Table Service
Price: $$$
Menu Items: shrimp, fried calamari, clam chowder, salads, fish, pasta, burgers, sandwiches
Recommendation: Crab Cake Sandwich, Shrimp Mac and Cheese, Lobster Roll

ILLUMINATION'S MINIONS CAFE

Minions Land
Description: A diner with three different segments: kitchen, break room, and dining room. In the break room, look for vending machines with "mischievous items."
Type: Quick Service
Price: $-$$
Menu Items: sandwiches, noodle bowls soup
Recommendation: Uncle Dru's Belly Fillin' Pork Sandwich

> · **Magic Tips** ·
> The Minions Cafe also has an express window with select items.

LOUIE'S ITALIAN RESTAURANT Ω ❤

New York
Description: Grab pizza by the slice or a sub at this cafeteria-style eatery. The ambiance is lackluster (feels like a dingy cafeteria), but the pizza is pretty good!

Type: Quick Service
Price: $-$$
Menu Items: pizzas, subs, chicken parmesan, pasta, Caesar salad
Recommendation: Jumbo Pizza Slice (any flavor) ❤

RICHTER'S BURGER CO. Ω

San Francisco
Description: Chow down on a burger of your choice in this swanky, wharf-themed cafeteria. We wish the burgers were better, but they're not terrible. Still, we'd recommend heading to the Hard Rock Café in CityWalk for a burger instead.
Type: Quick Service
Price: $-$$
Menu Items: burgers, chicken sandwiches, salads, fries, cheese fries, soda floats, shakes
Recommendation: Frisco Shake (chocolate or vanilla)

TODAY CAFE Ω

New York
Description: A great place for healthier options and breakfast items, including the special TODAY Show brewed coffee.
Type: Quick Service
Price: $-$$
Menu Items: breakfast sandwiches, breakfast bowls, pastries, sandwiches, salads, cheese plate, soda, tea, coffee
Recommendation: Al's Avocado Toast Sandwich

> **· Magic Tips ·**
> To save money on water, guests are allowed to bring their own refillable bottles into the parks. For refills, ask Team Members at Quick Service restaurants or Snack Carts with soda fountains. They'll provide free ice water cups for you to fill your bottle. However, they will not refill your bottle for you.

MORE EATS

Bake My Day ($) – Located in Minions Land. Purchase various flavored cupcakes, macarons, s'mores, and more!

Bumblebee Man's Taco Truck ($) – Located in Springfield. Try one of Bumblebee Man's crafted tacos, they come 2 per order right out of a taco truck. We recommend the juicy Korean Beef Taco for a delicious Asian-Mexican fusion.

Chez Alcatraz ($) – Located in San Francisco. Bar food and drinks in a hut by the wharf. The bartenders are usually fast pourers and attentive. However, on busy days, there likely won't be room to sit around this small area.

Duff Brewery ($) – Located in Springfield. Try a draft beer (ages 21 and older) in an outdoor brewing area inspired by *The Simpsons*.

Flaming Moe's ($) – Located in Springfield. Try draft beer (ages 21 and older) or a Flaming Moe ❤ (non-alcoholic) that fizzes as you drink it! The decor in Flaming Moe's looks just like its namesake in The Simpsons. You can even have a drink with Barney Gumble!

Florean Fortescue's Ice-Cream Parlour ($) – Located in Diagon Alley. *Harry Potter*-themed ice cream served in a waffle cone, cup, or souvenir glass. We recommend the Butterbeer soft serve or sticky toffee pudding!

Fountain of Fair Fortune ($) ❤– Located in Diagon Alley. Harry Potter-themed eats and drinks. Try the minty Fishy Green Ale!

Freeze Ray Pops ($) – Located in Minions Land. Various flavors of popsicles.

Häagen-Dazs ($) – Located in New York. Classic ice cream scoops from the famous brand.

The Hopping Pot ($) ❤– Located in Diagon Alley. *Harry Potter*-themed eats and drinks. Try the Butterbeer here. They also have a fine selection of alcoholic beers for those 21 and older. Try taking a sip of both Butterbeer and a draft beer at the same time—we love it!

Lard Lad Donuts ($) ❤– Located in Springfield. Donuts and more donuts! Try the Big Pink, an enormous donut with enough sweetness to feed a family!

Pop-A-Nana ($) – Located in Minions Land. A stand serving banana-flavored popcorn.

San Francisco Pastry Company ($-$$) **Ω** – Located in San Francisco. Daily baked breads to make sandwiches and baked goods. We recommend trying one of their tasty muffins.

Starbucks Coffee ($) – Located in New York. The world-famous brewing company brings its brand to Universal. Get your favorite drinks here.

ISLANDS OF ADVENTURE

BLONDIE'S Ω
Toon Lagoon
Description: Sandwiches made big enough to feed Dagwood from the Blondie comic strips. Similar to subway, you can style your own sub.
Type: Quick Service
Price: $$
Menu Items: sandwiches, hot dogs, potato salad
Recommendation: Dagwood Sandwich

THE BURGER DIGS Ω
Jurassic Park
Description: Serving up burgers and fries in this *Jurassic Park*-themed cafeteria. When choosing dining in Jurassic

Park, we prefer Thunder Falls Terrace over Burger Digs as we find the food and ambiance better.
Type: Quick Service
Price: $$
Menu Items: Burgers, fries, onion rings
Recommendation: Onion Rings

CAFE 4 Ω

Marvel Super Hero Island
Description: A pizza cafeteria styled after Marvel Comics' Fantastic 4. The inside looks like a 90s comic café, and the pizza is fairly good.
Type: Quick Service
Price: $$
Menu Items: pizza, Caesar salad, pasta, sandwiches
Recommendation: Pizza with your choice of toppings

CAPTAIN AMERICA DINER Ω

Marvel Super Hero Island
Description: A burger cafeteria styled after Marvel Comics' Captain America. The inside also looks a 90s comic café, and the burgers are just okay.
Type: Quick Service
Price: $$
Menu Items: burgers, salad, onion rings, fries, sandwiches, shakes
Recommendation: Onion Rings

CIRCUS MCGURKUS CAFE STOO-PENDOUS Ω ❤

Seuss Landing
Description: A brightly colored and well-themed diner in a Seuss-style circus tent! See your favorite Dr. Seuss characters as you dine on American favorites.
Type: Quick Service
Price: $$
Menu Items: pasta, fried chicken, burgers, salad, sandwiches, pizza, and ice cream
Recommendation: Fried Chicken Platter (comes in 2-piece and 3-piece) ❤

COMIC STRIP CAFE Ω
Toon Lagoon
Description: A burger and hot dog cafeteria with comic book decor. The food is just okay.
Type: Quick Service
Price: $$
Menu Items: burgers, hot dogs, salad, onion rings, fish, sandwiches, shakes
Recommendation: Fish and Chips, Onion Rings

CONFISCO GRILLE Ω ❤
Port of Entry
Description: Taste around the world with this hodgepodge of selections. Even the restaurant's décor amplifies a medley of cultures from around the world. From Italian and Mexican to Asian and American, there's something at Confisco for everyone. The food here is pretty good, and even better if you know what to order (see our recommendations).
Type: Table Service
Price: $$$
Menu Items: sandwiches, bowls, wraps, ribs, nachos, wings, quesadillas, hummus, salads, soda
Recommendation: Sweet and Sour Sticky Ribs, Pork Belly Banh-Mi Sandwich, Hearthstone Baked Chicken Sandwich

DOC SUGRUE'S KEBAB HOUSE Ω ❤
The Lost Continent
Description: Try a flavorful kebab and other Mediterranean cuisine at this delicious window-service eatery.
Type: Quick Service
Price: $$
Menu Items: chicken, beef, and vegetarian kebab skewers, Greek salad, hummus
Recommendation: All of the kebabs are very tasty ❤. The meat and vegetables are marinated and come with pita bread and Greek yogurt dipping sauce.

FIRE EATER'S GRILL Ω
The Lost Continent

Description: American and Greek favorites from a window-service eatery. Eat here if you're craving a chili cheese dog (though they aren't very flavorful), otherwise head to Doc Sugrue's in the Lost Continent as the food is better.
Type: Quick Service
Price: $-$$
Menu Items: chicken fingers, chili cheese dog, gyro, salads, chili cheese fries
Recommendation: Chicken Fingers

MYTHOS RESTAURANT Ω
The Lost Continent
Description: A wonderfully themed Mediterranean restaurant with popular food. There are cascading waterfalls and the perfectly detailed architecture all around. The menu has been refreshed with delicious salads, gnocchi, and more.
Type: Table Service
Price: $$$
Menu Items: flat bread, fried calamari, salad, pad thai, risotto, fish, Italian pasta, sandwiches, burger
Recommendation: Spanakopita Dip, Gnocchi Bolognese

· **Magic Tips** ·
Mythos is the most popular dining destination in the theme parks, so get a reservation before you go. Even on not-so-busy days, we've seen people wait hours to dine here. Book your reservation on Universal Orlando's website.

NATURAL SELECTIONS
Jurassic Park
Description: A small food cart with snacks, soda, and beer.
Type: Snack Cart
Price: $
Menu Items: empanadas, churros, fruit, soda, beer
Recommendation: Dulce de Leche Churro and Beef Empanada

PIZZA PREDATTORIA Ω

Jurassic Park

Description: Grab a slice of pizza in this outdoor picnic area. The pizza is pretty good.

Type: Quick Service

Price: $$

Menu Items: pizza, meatball subs, salads

Recommendation: Meat Lovers Pizza

THREE BROOMSTICKS Ω ❤

Hogsmeade

Description: Our favorite dining spot in the Universal Orlando Resort! The *Harry Potter* homages in this restaurant are magical and the food is very tasty. There's often a short line before ordering, which can be handy for indecisive diners. The food is on display in windows for you to see how it's prepared. Once you order, you'll wait for your tray and then the dining staff will find you a table. This way, you always know that you're sitting somewhere with enough seats and that it's been properly cleaned before you dine!

Type: Quick Service

Price: $$

Menu Items: fish and chips, Cornish pasties, spare ribs, chicken, turkey leg, salads, shepherd's pie, Butterbeer, *Harry Potter*-themed desserts

Recommendation: We've enjoyed every item on this menu, but our favorites include the Chicken and Ribs Platter ❤, Fish & Chips, and Cornish Pasties (they are sort of like empanadas). For dessert, try the Butterbeer Potted Cream ❤ (a pudding-like delicious dessert flavored like Butterbeer)

· Magic Tips ·

If you're planning on lunch at Three Broomsticks on a busy day, we recommend getting there by 11:30am to avoid the lunch rush. For later lunching, head there after 2:30pm. Dinner at Three Broomsticks isn't as popular as midday dining.

THUNDER FALLS TERRACE Ω ❤
Jurassic Park
Description: One of the better-themed dining experiences, Thunder Falls Terrace has views of the River Adventure as boats drop down. Order savory BBQ and American favorites here.
Type: Quick Service
Price: $$
Menu Items: BBQ ribs, chicken, wraps, burgers, salads, soups
Recommendation: Chicken & Ribs ❤

WIMPY'S Ω
Toon Lagoon
Description: Burgers and fries served counter style. You can get a combination meal served with a slice of apple pie. This restaurant is seasonal and may only open during the holiday season.
Type: Quick Service
Price: $$
Menu Items: burgers, fries, onion rings, apple pie
Recommendation: Apple Pie

MORE EATS

Backwater Bar ($-$$) ❤ – Located in Port of Entry. A full service "dive bar" (it's not actually a dive, but made to look like one) serving up tasty specialty cocktails and wine for those 21 and older. This is one of our favorite spots when traveling with adults!

Cinnabon ($) – Located in Port of Entry. A chain bakery serving up their famously delicious cinnamon rolls.

Croissant Moon Bakery ($) **Ω** – Located in Port of Entry. A great place to grab a muffin for breakfast. However, if not fresh, their food items can be pretty bland.

Green Eggs and Ham Cafe ($) **Ω** – Located in Seuss Landing. This dining station is only open seasonally (typically during the Holiday season) and offers tots (fried potatoes) with different toppings. We recommend the Pizza Tots or the Green Eggs & Ham Tots.

Hog's Head ($-$$) ❤ – Located in Hogsmeade. Try Butterbeer or a Harry Potter mixed drink or beer (for those 21 and older). The decor is very cool in here with the moving hog's head placed on the wall. We recommend the Pear Dazzle, a vodka-based mixed drink with a lightly sweet flavor. For the kids, have them try a Pumpkin Juice out of the bottle or Butterbeer.

Hop On Pop Ice Cream Shop ($) – Located in Seuss Landing. Frozen treats styled after Dr. Seuss' books. Try a Brownie Sundae in a Waffle Bowl.

Moose Juice, Goose Juice ($) – Located in Seuss Landing. Snacks and drinks inspired by the imaginative creatures of Dr. Seuss. Try their Goose Juice (a frozen sour green apple blended beverage).

Starbucks Coffee ($) – Located in Port of Entry. The world-famous coffee company brings its brand to Islands of Adventure. Get your favorite drinks here.

The Watering Hole ($-$$) – Located in Jurassic Park. Those 21 and older can grab a draft beer or mixed drink here. They also serve nachos and pretzels, but the food often tastes stale.

VOLCANO BAY

Bambu ($-$$) **Ω** – Burgers, hot dogs, chicken tenders, and salads. We recommend trying the Pretzel Dog. The Pineapple Upside Down Cake is very good, too.

Dancing Dragons Boat Bar ($) – Spot this bar by looking for the sails printed with floral designs. A perfect place to grab an island-inspired mixed drink (for those 21 and older).

The Feasting Frog ($-$$) **Ω** – A frog-shaped hut serving tacos and poke bowls. The plantain chips and guacamole are a delicious surprise!

Kunuku Boat Bar ($) – Fruit-infused specialty drinks and beers (for those 21 and older). The drinks can be a bit sugary.

Kohola Reef Restaurant & Social Club ($$) **Ω ❤** – Grab lunch at this oasis-style restaurant. The Mango BBQ Pulled Pork Sandwich packs some great flavor.

Whakawaiwai Eats ($-$$) **Ω ❤** – Quick service flatbreads that are delicious! We recommend stopping by here for a bite.

· Magic Tips ·
Remember that you can link your credit card to your TapuTapu bracelet using the Universal Orlando app! This feature, called "TapTu Pay," makes it easier for walking around the water park and paying for items as needed.

CITYWALK DINING

ANTOJITOS AUTHENTIC MEXICAN FOOD Ω ❤
Description: A delicious Mexican dining experience with live music.
Type: Table service
Open: Dinner
Price: $$ – $$$

Review: Antojitos is certainly one of the better restaurants in Universal Orlando. We love the south-of-the-border ambiance with colorful décor, friendly staff, and mariachi music playing around the restaurant. We're perhaps a bit snobbish when it comes to Mexican food, and their menu choices are very, very good! In the evenings, especially on weekends, live musicians hit the stage to perform. If you're just stopping in for a drink, they have an extensive tequila selection. During the week, you likely won't need a reservation, but weekends and holidays, we recommend one. Call (407) 224-3663 to reserve.

Menu Items: Mexican-style foods—chips and guacamole, nachos, beans, quesadillas, taco salad, enchiladas, fajitas, tacos, carnitas, burritos, chimichangas, tortilla soup, margaritas, tequila, cocktails, soda

For Kids: Tacos, quesadillas, empanadas, grilled chicken breast

Recommendations: Chimichanga (fried burrito stuffed with marinated chicken, cheese, salsa, guacamole, and served with black beans and rice), Fajitas (choose from chicken, vegetable, carne, or a combination of two. Freshly grilled on a skillet and served with warm, house-made tortillas, guacamole, sour cream, cheese, and pico de gallo).

Adults (21 and older): Try any of their margaritas.

BIGFIRE

Description: American favorites cooked over a massive wood-burning fire.

Type: Table Service

Open: Dinner

Price: $$$

Review: A fun concept for diners looking for something a little different. Get steaks, burgers, and more cooked over a giant "bigfire" grill in the restaurant. Each meal is placed on a piece of wood—cherry, pecan, or oak—to give added flavor to the dish being cooked. The menu is a bit like one you'd find at a steakhouse, but the theatrics of the big fire make it something much more fun.

Menu Items: Steaks, seafood, fried chicken, burgers, fish, lamb chops, salads, desserts, wine, beer, sodas

Kids: chicken fingers, sliders, mac and cheese, steak, chicken and beef skewers, juice, chocolate milk, milk, root beer
Recommendation: Steak, Bison Burger, Pork Belly Mac & Cheese (side), S'mores (dessert)

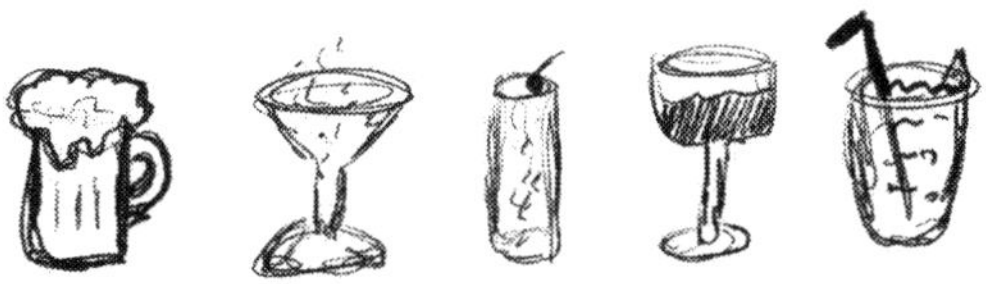

BOB MARLEY A TRIBUTE TO FREEDOM Ω
Description: Jamaican dining with live reggae styled after Bob Marley
Type: Table Service and Dance Bar
Open: Dinner and Late Night
Price: $$
Review: Eat, drink, and dance the night away to live reggae in this unique setting. The food isn't remarkable, so we recommending visiting for the small club scene. Bob Marley's has an event nearly every night of the week. The dinner menu is famous for "belly full" items that make you feel stuffed.
Menu Items: Jamaican jerk chicken, salad, lamb skewers, oxtail stew, curry chicken, fish, sodas, full bar
For Kids: Mac and cheese, chicken tenders, burger with rice
Recommendation: Reggae Jamaican Jerk Chicken
Adults (21 and older): Caribbean Calamity – Bacardi rum and banana liqueur with orange and pineapple juices

BUBBA GUMP SHRIMP CO. ❤
Description: *Forrest Gump*-themed dining with plenty of shrimp and American favorites
Type: Table Service
Open: Lunch and Dinner
Price: $$
Review: The restaurant from *Forrest Gump* comes to life with some very delicious food! Bubba Gump's has fun waiters,

themed rooms from the movie, and unforgettable food. If you're a fan of fried shrimp, we highly recommend this place. However, the fried chicken is especially good, too. Before you order, your waiter asks *Forrest Gump* trivia—it's a lot of fun, even if you haven't seen the movie in years. As far as chain restaurants go, Bubba Gump wins the prize for overall customer satisfaction from us.

Menu Items: Burger, shrimp, salad, clam chowder, sandwiches, fried chicken, cocktails, beer, wine, soda

For Kids: hamburger, hot dog, chicken fingers

Recommendation: Shrimpers Heaven ❤ – breaded coconut shrimp, chilly shrimp, fried shrimp, and tempura shrimp served with fries and dipping sauce. It's a lot of food, but shrimp lovers will be in heaven. Mama's Southern Fried Chicken – tastes like a homemade southern boneless chicken meal. Served with mashed potatoes, gravy, and corn.

Adult (21 and older): Lava Flow – a sweet mix of rum, coconut cream, strawberries, banana, and pineapple juice. The glass is large and tastes like a smoothie with rum.

THE COWFISH Ω

Description: A clever name! The Cow stands for burgers and the Fish stands for sushi. Grab either at this trendy dining joint.

Type: Table service

Open: Lunch and Dinner

Price: $$–$$$

Review: Cowfish has great service and an interesting combination of dining options. This restaurant concept is sort of genius because there's something for everyone. The sushi lovers will get their fill and those just craving a great burger will feel satisfied. This multi-level building is known for its decent-sized portions and crafty menu options. We used to love sushi and burgers, but we haven't been impressed with the quality recently. Their signature dish, Burgushi—where they mix sushi and hamburgers—sounded strange at first. However, they're probably their best rolls.

Menu Items: Sushi, burgers, salads, calamari, edamame, sandwiches, cocktails, wine, beer, shakes, soda, desserts

For Kids: Chicken nuggets, grilled cheese, PB&J, mac and cheese, mini burgers, sushi
Recommendation:
The All-American Bacon Double Cheeseburgooshi

HARD ROCK CAFE ORLANDO

Description: An American restaurant with rock 'n' roll memorabilia.
Type: Table service
Open: Breakfast, Lunch, and Dinner
Price: $$
Review: The world-famous restaurant chain finds its Colosseum-shaped home in Orlando. We love the Hard Rock Cafe's exterior with weathered, Roman amphitheater structure. There's a sort of fun, larger-than-life Vegas feel to this multi-level diner. Like most other Hard Rock Cafes, the food is mostly burgers, sodas, and alcohol. Still, the restaurant serves one of the better burgers at the Universal Orlando Resort.
Menu Items:
Breakfast: eggs, bacon, omelet, chicken and waffles, French toast, waffle, mimosas, bloody mary, coffee, soda
Lunch and Dinner: burgers, sandwiches, salad, nacho, wings, potato skins, barbecue, shakes, desserts, cocktails, beer, wine, soda
Kids: hamburger, hot dog, chicken tenders, fish sticks, mac and cheese, cheese pizza, pasta, chicken breast, root beer float
Recommendation:
Breakfast: Chicken and Waffles
Lunch and Dinner: Hickory Barbecue Bacon Cheeseburger
Dessert: Hot Fudge Brownie, served with vanilla ice cream with melted hot fudge. The apple cobbler is pretty good, too!

JIMMY BUFFET'S MARGARITAVILLE Ω

Description: An island-themed dining experience with nightly live music.
Type: Table service
Open: Lunch, Dinner and Late Night
Price: $$

Review: Margaritaville brings nightly live music, great drinks, and tasty offerings to CityWalk. The live music is great with rock and pop covers, and the bar has friendly staff. The food is pretty good, too. Nothing fancy, just a good time with burgers, fries, seafood, and plenty to drink. Kids also like Margaritaville because of the lively atmosphere.

Menu Items: Burgers, salads, sandwiches, tacos, shrimp, fish, fried chicken, steak, seafood mac and cheese, chicken breast, vegetarian, beer, wine, cocktails, margaritas

For Kids: Burger, fish and chips, fried shrimp, chicken strips, pasta, mac and cheese

Recommendation: Fish Tacos, Crispy Coconut Shrimp, or Cheeseburger in Paradise

Adults (21 and older): Who's to Blame Margarita

Live Shows: There are two bars at Margaritaville. The inside one can get a bit packed, so if you're just looking for a margarita, try the outdoor one. Both are excellent choices for drinks. You can find the band schedule at their website: **www.margaritavilleorlando.com**

NBC SPORTS GRILL Ω

Description: A New American restaurant with sports TV.

Type: Table service

Open: Lunch, Dinner, and Late Night (1:30am)

Price: $$–$$$

Review: The flashy, large televisions on the outside of the NBC Sports Grill are certainly eye catching. Even if you don't like sports, you'll likely want to check out the commotion. However, NBC Sports Grill is strictly for the sport fans. The food is pretty good and the inside just looks like a chain restaurant with televisions.

Menu Items: Sliders, burgers, fried calamari, poutine, nachos, wings, lettuce wraps, salad, steak, sandwich, fish tacos, pasta, desserts, beer, full bar, cocktails, wine, soda

For Kids: hamburger, hot dog, chicken tenders, fish sticks, mac and cheese, cheese pizza, pasta, chicken breast, root beer float

Recommendation:

Appetizer: Wisconsin Cheese Curds – fried cheddar and spicy tomato jam

Entrees: Wisconsin Burger – It's all in the cheese! Cheddar, thick bacon, lettuce, tomato, and a brioche bun. Also comes with your choice of fries or tots.

PAT O'BRIEN'S ORLANDO Ω
Description: A dueling piano Cajun restaurant and bar
Type: Table service
Open: Dinner and Late Night Music Bar
Price: $$–$$$
Review: Step onto Bourbon Street at this brick house filled with dueling pianos, a full bar, and even a water fountain with fire! If you're into the dueling piano scene, where two piano players face off in song, Pat O'Brien's is your place. The food is nothing to write home about, but they pour strong drinks! The bar is often open late (2am) nightly. If you visit after 9pm, you may have to pay a cover fee.
Menu Items: Steak, pasta, fish, salad, gumbo, jambalaya, crawfish, burger, andouille sausage, chicken, mint julep, beer, wine, mixed drinks
For Kids: hamburger, hot dog, chicken fingers
Recommendation: We haven't loved anything here, but the O'Brien's Burger and N' Awlin's Po-Boy are decent.

RED OVEN PIZZA BAKERY Ω
Description: Contemporary pizza table service restaurant.
Type: Quick Service
Open: Lunch and Dinner
Price: $$
Review: If you're craving pizza, this is the best spot in the Universal Orlando Resort. The slices look like they came right out of a New York pizza spot with creamy melted mozzarella and large pepperonis. The fun of Red Oven is watching the chefs toss the dough to make the pizzas. A pie runs about $13 and is big enough for one person. They also have smaller pizzas for kids.
Menu Items: Pizza, salad, beer, wine, soda
For Kids: chicken fingers, mini burgers, pasta, chicken with rice, waffle
Recommendation: Prosciutto and Arugula Pizza

TOOTHSOME CHOCOLATE EMPORIUM

Description: Sweets and dishes in a steampunk theme.
Type: Table service and dessert bar
Open: Lunch and Dinner (also serves Brunch all day)
Price: $$–$$$
Review: The theme is like Charlie and the Chocolate Factory meets 19th century steampunk. The decor is stunning and the food looks mouthwatering. For mechanical gears to wild costumes, there's plenty to see around the room while you wait for a seat. We love looking at the array of desserts like fancy chocolates. Once seated, you'll have to resist ordering a little bit of everything. Since Toothsome's best designs are sweets, we recommend getting the brunch for lunch or dinner (they serve it all day).
Menu Items: Flatbreads, salads, soups, sandwiches, hamburgers, pasta, chicken, steak, crepes, quiche, waffles, French toast, milkshakes, desserts, beer, full bar, cocktails, wine, soda
For Kids: chicken fingers, mini burgers, pasta, chicken with rice, waffle
Recommendation:
Appetizer: Philly Cheesesteak Rolls
Entrees: Blackened Steak and Blue Flatbread – blue cheese, steak, caramelized onions, mushrooms, and spinach. Very flavorful!

> **Note:** Toothsome also serves all-day brunch with sweet crepes and waffles that are worth ordering!

VIVO ITALIAN KITCHEN Ω ❤

Description: Trendy Italian table service.
Type: Table Service
Open: Lunch and Dinner
Price: $$–$$$
Review: There are two great Italian choices in the Resort: Mama Della's Ristorante in the Portofino Bay Hotel and Vivo Italian Kitchen in CityWalk. While Mama Della's gives a more authentic Italian vibe, Vivo brings the trendy atmosphere. Try anything from pizza to pasta and Caesar salad to swordfish.

Menu Items: Pizza, pasta, salad, bolognese, lasagna, fish, chicken, lamb, wine, beer, specialty drinks, soda
For Kids: spaghetti and meatball, pizza, chicken breast, shrimp skewer, meatball sandwiches
Recommendation: Their pasta dishes are delicious!

MORE EATS

Auntie Anne's Pretzels ($) – Delicious soft pretzels. We recommend the Cinnamon Sugar Nuggets (pretzel bits covered in cinnamon and sugar).

Bend the Bao ($) – Bao buns filled with delicious Asian-fusion bites. Try Pork Belly Bao or Veggie Bao at this tasty (and colorful) snack station.

Bread Box Handcrafted Sandwiches ($-$$) **Ω** – A corner store deli with handmade sandwiches. These are pretty good, especially the BLTA – bacon, arugula, tomato, balsamic mayonnaise, avocado sandwich.

Cinnabon ($) – Delectable warm and frosted cinnamon rolls

Cold Stone Creamery ($) – Ice cream made to order.

Fat Tuesday ($) – Alcoholic smoothie counter (for those 21 and older). Some of these can be extremely sweet, but we recommend the Peach bellini.

Hot Dog Hall of Fame ($-$$) **Ω** – Creative hot dogs inspired by the ball parks. Italian Sausage (with provolone, grilled onions, and peppers) is tasty!

Menchie's Frozen Yogurt ($) – Self-serve froyo.

Moe's Southwest Grill ($-$$) – Tex Mex Counter Service. Try the Homewrecker Burrito – a huge burrito stuffed with rice, beans, cheese, pico de gallo, guacamole, and sour cream. We recommend it with chicken or steak.

Panda Express ($-$$) – Quick to order Chinese food. Their glazed orange chicken is one of the best in the world.

Starbucks ($) – America's top choice for coffee.

Whopper Bar by Burger King ($-$$) – Burger King's more upscale flame-broiled burgers. Try the Bourbon Burger, a beef patty with cheddar, bourbon sauce, and onion rings.

Voodoo Doughnut ($) ❤ – Grab a specialty donut inspired by Universal films. These desserts are delicious and Voodoo is open late, until midnight on weekdays and 1am on the weekends.

HOTEL DINING

HARD ROCK HOTEL

BEACHCLUB
Description: Poolside bar and grill.
Type: Table service and bar
Open: Lunch and Dinner
Price: $$
Review: The Beachclub is an excellent choice for casual dining. No shirt? No problem! The waiters and bartenders serve those dressed or in their swimsuits. Oh, and the drinks are very delicious!
Menu Items: nachos, wings, quesadilla, loaded fries, ahi tuna, cheese sticks, pizza, egg roll, chips and salsa, edamame, tacos, burgers, wraps, hot dogs, smoothies, cocktails, and soda
For Kids: pizza, grilled cheese, mini burger, mac and cheese
Adult Beverages: mojitos, spiked lemonade, various cocktails, spiked slushies, margaritas, beer, wines, bloody mary

Recommendation: Loaded Nachos – tortilla chips, cheese, lettuce, tomato, sour cream, guacamole, pico de gallo, and optional chicken or beef.

THE KITCHEN

Description: New American cuisine with a 50s high-end rock diner feel.

Type: Table service

Open: Breakfast, Lunch, Dinner

Price: $$ – $$$

Review: Delicious American food with friendly waiters and a restaurant that's fun to experience. The music is great and the prices aren't too shabby. For breakfast, they offer a buffet or a la carte. Kids under 3 eat at the buffet for free with a paying adult. The lunch and dinner menus are very similar in portion and price. If you're looking for something different, try the gator tail—it's surprisingly flavorful!

Menu Items:

Breakfast: omelet station, griddle station, muffins, pastries, breakfast pizza, yogurt, cottage cheese, scrambled eggs, biscuits and gravy, waffles, pancakes, bacon, sausage, sticky buns, corned beef hash, fruit, cereal, grits, oatmeal

Lunch and Dinner: Flatbreads, pasta, spinach and artichoke dip, soup, calamari, gator tail, quesadilla, burger, chicken and waffle, tacos, chicken potpie, short ribs, steak, shrimp, ahi tuna, cocktails, soda

For Kids: grilled cheese, hot dog, fries, turkey sandwich, pb&j sandwich, burger, pizza, chicken tenders

Recommendation: The Kitchen Burger: Angus beef, bacon, cheddar, onion rings, lettuce, tomato, and chipotle aioli. It's big and good!

· Magic Tips ·

The Kitchen Sink Challenge: A guest who eats the Kitchen Burger, 1 pound of fries, a fried pickle, and a 7-layer Kitchen Sink Cake in under 30 minutes, gets a free meal on the house. Ask your waiter about this!

PALM RESTAURANT ❤

Description: American steakhouse.
Type: Table service
Open: Dinner
Price: $$ – $$$
Review: If you're looking for a bit more of an upscale affair, put Palm Steakhouse on your list. Serving up turf and surf, you can enjoy everything from mouthwatering steak to succulent lobsters. The food and the staff here are fantastic and steak lovers will leave very satisfied. The Palm also has a wide variety of wines and a full bar. We wish the décor was a little bit more fun, but the classic 1920s atmosphere is fun enough with your savory meal.
Menu Items: steak, lobster, salad, Italian, seafood, vegetables, and dessert. Also a variety of wines, cocktails, and soda.
For Kids: mozzarella sticks, steak, fries, mac and cheese, cheeseburger, grilled cheese sandwich, pasta, chicken strips
Recommendation: Filet Mignon, House Specialty Nova Scotia Lobster, or both with the Surf and Turf
Dress Code: Palm asks that guests come in resort or business casual wear, as sleeveless shirts and beachwear are not permitted.

MORE EATS

Room Service – Get American favorite dishes delivered right to your room! Hard Rock's room service is great, but can get a little slow late at night. Just keep in mind that delivery can take an hour or so.

PORTOFINO BAY

BICE RISTORANTE

Description: Traditional Italian.

Type: Upscale table service
Open: Dinner
Price: $$$
Review: A perfect intimate scene that transports you to Italy. Friendly staff serve delicious Italian food in an authentic way with several courses. Though the menu is similar to Mama Della's, the food has a different flare of seasonings. Come in cocktail or business casual attire. We prefer Mama Della's because the prices are better than Bice and we think the food is tastier. However, if you're looking for an upscale dining experience, Bice won't disappoint. Don't worry if you can't pronounce the words, the waiters are used to it and happy that you tried your best!
Menu Items: Pasta, soup, antipasta, insalate, veal, steak, Italian desserts, wine, soda
Recommendation: Anitpasto all'Italiana con Salumi, Ravioli di Manzo all Massaia, Petto Di Pollo Ripieno di Fontina, Crème Cotta alla Vaniglia – vanilla crème brule

MAMA DELLA'S RISTORANTE ❤
Description: Homestyle Italian restaurant.
Type: Table service
Open: Dinner
Price: $$$
Review: One of the best restaurants on the Resort! We love Mama Della's for its tasty Italian cuisine, charming performers, and overall aesthetics. Perfect for special occasions, let the singers serenade you in the intimate venue—a few dollars in cash tips are recommended. The menu keeps pretty close to homestyle American Italian meals, so come hungry!
Menu Items: Pasta, soup, calamari, scampi, caprese, antipasto, ravioli, cabonara, gnocchi, eggplant parmesan, lasagna, vegetarian, wine, soda
For Kids: macaroni and cheese, fettuccine alfredo, spaghetti and meatballs, pizza, peanut butter and jelly sandwich, buttered noodles and ham, lasagna, chicken fingers
Recommendations: Calamari fritti, Gnocchi al Pomodoro or Lasagna ❤, Tiramisu

TRATTORIA DEL PORTO

Description: Family Italian and American breakfast.

Type: American and Italian Casual Dining

Open: Breakfast, Lunch and Dinner

Price: $$

Review: One of the better restaurants for the whole family. Dine on Italian favorites and meet some characters like the Minions from *Despicable Me*. The environment is much more casual than the other Portofino Bay restaurants, so everyone can feel relaxed as they enjoy some good food.

Menu Items:

Breakfast: baked goods, eggs, bacon, hash browns, pancakes, waffles, French toast, eggs benedict, breakfast wraps, steak and eggs, custom omelets, smoothies, fruit, oatmeal, cereal, banana split, juice

Lunch: soup, salad, flatbread, sandwiches, burgers, pasta, dessert, wine, beer, soda

Dinner: soup, salad, flatbread, sandwiches, burgers, pasta, steak, swordfish, shrimp and grits, salmon, dessert, wine, beer, soda

For Kids: quesadilla, hot dog, French fries, pizza, chicken fingers, peanut butter and jelly, cheeseburger, steak, fettuccini alfredo, punch

Recommendation:

Breakfast: Eggs Beneditto – eggs, prosciutto, arugula, and hollandaise on ciabatta bread

Lunch: Citrus Marinated Chicken Sandwich – lettuce, tomatoes, pepper jack cheese, aioli

Dinner: Grilled Chicken Sandwich – lettuce, tomatoes, cheddar, bacon, aioli

> **Note:** For character dining, visit Friday nights from 6:30pm – 9:30pm.

MORE EATS

Room Service – Open 24 hours a day, 7 days a week with American favorites from burgers to pizza and kids' items, too.

Sal's Market Deli – Pizzas and Italian made to order. Try the prosciutto or Margherita pizza. The large is perfect for sharing! Fast and inexpensive compared to the table service places.

Splendido Bar and Grill – A poolside bar and grill with a lax environment. Stroll in for a drink, burger, or salad.

Gelateria – Sample from several types of gelato. Pick your favorite and stroll the waterway.

Starbucks - America's #1 coffee chain is open daily from 6am – 8pm

ROYAL PACIFIC

JAKE'S AMERICAN BAR

Description: American Favorites and full bar
Type: Casual table service
Open: Lunch and Dinner
Price: $$
Menu Items: cheese board, calamari, hot wings, cheese fries, salad, soup, burgers, sandwiches, chicken, fish and chips, steak, pasta, short ribs, pizza, full bar, soda, wine, cocktails
Kids: burger, sandwich, quesadilla, fries, chicken tenders
Late Night: beef and cheese fries, bacon burger, Caesar salad, hot wings, pizzas
Review: Jake's feels like a place someone who owns a propeller plane or a boat might like to hang out after work. It's a relaxed island vibe centered around a full bar with a lot of choices. The food isn't as good as the high price suggests. Expect to pay $15-$30 for an entrée, but these *are* amusement park prices. Jake's wins points for being open late with a late-night menu that's not too pricey.
Recommendation: B-1 Bomber Burger (standard burger with bacon)

ORCHID COURT LOUNGE & SUSHI BAR

Description: Casual sushi bar in a lounge setting.
Type: Japanese
Open: Lunch and Dinner
Price: $$
Review: A simple sushi bar inside of the hotel. Focuses mostly around the drinks, but you can get rolls ordered at a decent price. The rolls are pretty tasty!

BULA BAR AND GRILL

Description: Our door bar with food.
Type: American and Polynesian
Open: Lunch and Dinner
Price: $$
Review: A simple outdoor bar near the pool. Come dressed in your casual or pool clothing and order a drink or something to eat. The food is quite good, though we recommend sticking with standards like sliders, quesadilla, or a burger for the better flavors.

MORE EATS

Room Service – Open 24 hours a day, 7 days a week with American favorites from burgers to pizza and kids' items, too.

SAPPHIRE FALLS

AMATISTA COOKHOUSE

Description: Caribbean and American dining in a contemporary setting.
Type: Table service
Open: Breakfast, Lunch, and Dinner
Price: $$-$$$
Review: With a blend of ocean and land dishes, Amatista Cookhouse aims at the trendy, almost posh vibe you'd find in Miami or Los Angeles. Yet, the décor is simple, so dining here doesn't feel as exclusive as big city restaurants. The food is

decent, but nothing too special. You'll get the typical food found around Universal Orlando, so you may want to head to CityWalk or the Drhum Club Kantine pool bar with similar yet less expensive food. Still, there are some great dishes here. We recommend Amatista for breakfast, too.

Menu Items:

Breakfast: eggs, bacon, omelet, fruit, granola, pancakes, waffles, French toast, smoked salmon, cereal, muffin, juice, tea, coffee, soda

Lunch and Dinner: wings, empanadas, chowder, salad, fries, pizza, flatbread, pork chop, steak, burger, sandwiches

Recommendation:

Breakfast: Caribbean French toast

Lunch or Dinner: Amatista Caribbean Burger

DRHUM CLUB KANTINE

Description: Snacks and drink spot.

Price: $$

Type: Casual table service

Open: Lunch and Dinner

Review: Head outside and dine on tasty bar snacks and meals.

Menu Items:

Lunch and Dinner: Nachos, wings, empanadas, salad, fish, burgers, sandwiches, ice cream, margaritas, full bar

Kids: chicken fingers, grilled cheese, burger, hot dog

Recommendation: Nachos or Fish Taco

MORE EATS

New Dutch Trading Co. – Grab ice cream, smoothies, shakes, and even sandwiches, cake, and donuts from this snack stop.

Strong Water Tavern – A collection of vintage rums to dazzle adult senses. You can also try several tapas from around the world to pair with your choice of drink. As the bartender what he recommends! There's always something new to try.

Room Service – Open 24 hours a day, 7 days a week with American favorites from burgers to pizza and kids' items, too.

CABANA BAY

BAYLINER DINER

Description: Swanky quick-service eatery.
Price: $-$$
Type: Quick Service
Open: Breakfast, Lunch and Dinner
Review: Grab something quick and tasty here!
Menu Items:
Breakfast: pancakes, French toast, omelet, waffle, croissant, bagels, doughnuts, fruit salad, yogurt parfait, bacon, sausage
Lunch & Dinner: sandwiches, pizza, pasta, burgers, fries
Kids: pizza, pasta, burgers, fries, mac and cheese
Recommendation: Honolulu Hot Dog or Turkey Club Wrap

GALAXY BOWL RESTAURANT

Description: American dining in a swanky bowling alley.
Type: Quick Service
Open: Lunch and Dinner from 11am – 10pm
Review: Family friendly cuisine to match with your day or night of bowling. The food is pretty good and a great price.
Price: $-$$
Menu Items: Burgers, wraps, sandwiches, wings, quesadillas, pizza, soda, mixed drinks, beer, wine
Kids: chicken fingers, grilled cheese, mac and cheese
Recommendation: Ultimate Grilled Cheese Sandwich

THE HIDEAWAY BAR AND GRILLE

Description: Mid-century bar with food.
Price: $$
Type: Poolside
Open: Lunch and Dinner
Review: Hang by the pool and dine on American favorites.
Menu Items: Hot dogs, salads, fries, sandwiches, wraps, burgers, soda, juice, cocktails, beer

Kids: chicken fingers, grilled cheese, burger, fish sticks, peanut butter and jelly sandwich
Recommendation: Honolulu Hot Dog or Turkey Club Wrap

MORE EATS

Starbucks – Coffee, pastries, and breakfast items.

Atomic Tonic – An outdoor bar with specialty drinks and sandwiches, wraps, salads, and skewers. Try the delicious Cabana Bay Colada!

Delizioso Pizza – Pick up or order a pizza pie delivered to your room. Pizzas are about 10" and deliver from 10am – midnight, and until 1am on weekends. Call (407) 503-4300

Room Service – Open 24 hours a day, 7 days a week with American favorites from burgers to pizza and kids' items, too.

AVENTURA HOTEL

BAR 17 BISTRO

Description: Rooftop dining and bar.
Price: $-$$
Type: Table Service
Open: Snacks and Dinner from 5pm - 10pm, Drinks from 4pm - 2am (though it may close early on less popular nights)
Review: Adult-oriented dining and full bar.
Menu Items: burgers, salmon, steak, chicken, salads, chicken wings, Brussels sprouts, full bar
Recommendation: Rooftop Burger, Korean Fried Chicken Wings

URBAN PANTRY

Description: American, Asian, and European-inspired dining.
Price: $$
Type: Quick Service

Open: Breakfast, Lunch, and Dinner
Review: Urban Pantry offers a wider variety of bites not usually offered in the Universal Orlando Resort. There's something for everyone here.
Menu Items:
Breakfast: omelets, breakfast sandwiches, pastries, continental breakfast items, flatbreads, full bar
Lunch & Dinner: build-your-own wok, tuna poke, sushi, pizza, burgers, paella, chicken, carving station, full bar
Kids: chicken fingers, grilled cheese, burger, fish sticks, peanut butter and jelly sandwich
Recommendation: Build-your-own wok or a burger

MORE EATS

Starbucks – Coffee, pastries, and breakfast items

Bar Sol – A poolside bar

barVentura – A lobby lounge bar

Room Service – Open 24 hours a day, 7 days a week with American favorites from burgers to pizza and kids' items, too. You can order from the tablet in your room!

SURFSIDE INN

BEACH BREAK CAFE
Description: Fast-service inexpensive restaurant
Price: $-$$
Type: Quick-Service
Open: Breakfast, Lunch, and Dinner
Review: A California-style quick-service diner that boasts $12 or less menu items. Grab a quick burger or burrito here.
Menu Items:
Breakfast: eggs, bacon, pancakes, breakfast pizza (with eggs, sausage, bacon, and potatoes), breakfast burritos

Lunch/Dinner: sandwiches, salads, chicken, fish, burgers, chicken sandwich, fries, sodas, beers

MORE EATS

Starbucks – Coffee, pastries, and breakfast items

Sand Bar – A poolside bar

Pizza Delivery – Have a pizza delivered right to your room by calling on the provided phone.

DOCKSIDE INN

PIER 8 MARKET

Description: Casual food court with quick and easy dining options.
Price: $$
Type: Quick-Service
Open: Breakfast, Lunch, and Dinner
Review: Dine there or grab and go with delicious bites found in this food court.
Menu Items:
Breakfast: breakfast sandwiches, pancakes, avocado toast, breakfast pizzas, Chicken & Waffles, pastries, Krispy Kreme Doughnuts, juice, coffee, tea
Lunch & Dinner: sandwiches, salads, burgers, pizzas, Chicken & Waffles, fries, onion rings, desserts, soda, coffee, tea, juice
Grab-N-Go Options: sandwiches, salads, yogurt, fruit, desserts

MORE EATS

Coffee Shop – Coffee, tea, and snacks

Pool Bar – A poolside bar

CHAPTER ELEVEN

HALLOWEEN HORROR NIGHTS

INTRODUCTION

If Halloween is one of your favorite holidays, it might be time to book a trip to Universal Studios Orlando in autumn! Halloween Horror Nights is an epic, park-wide scare zone with haunted mazes, creepy treats, spooky stage shows—and so much more! Mostly popular with adults, the park transforms at sundown into a terrifying and ghastly world! You'll see your favorite horror movies and scary TV series come to life in this unique experience.

Halloween Horror Nights (HHN) is a separate ticketed nighttime event that takes place in just one of the parks (usually Universal Studios, but sometimes Islands of Adventure). Most of the rides are open with the addition of haunted mazes. Starting at the entrance, creepy demons and "serial killers" roam foggy streets. Each year holds a new set of terrifying surprises.

WHEN IS HHN?

The event takes place from mid-September through the first week of November. Tickets sell out faster closer to Halloween.

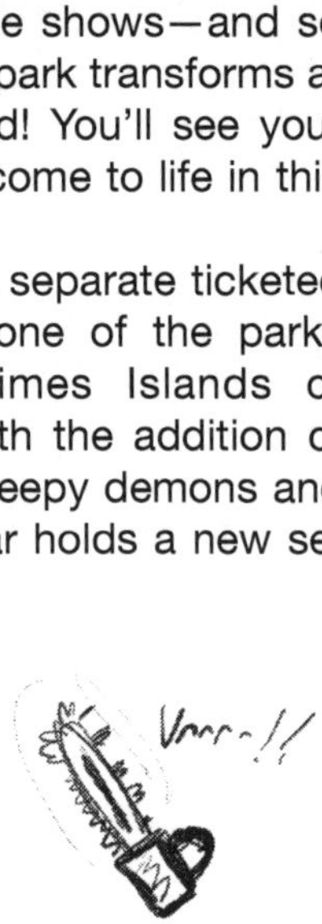

WHAT ARE THE SCARE ZONES AND MAZES?
Scare Zones and Mazes are frightening areas where horror franchises come to life. You might be chased by a chainsaw-wielding Jason or escape the wrath of killers from *The Purge* series. *American Horror Story, Nightmare on Elm Street, The Walking Dead, The Shining*, and *Saw* have all made appearances at HHN. Universal usually begins announcing maze and scare zone themes in the summer before the event.

SHOULD I BRING MY CHILD?
Probably not. Even if your kid can handle watching a horror movie, they might feel way too scared when a gang of nightmarish creatures chases them down the street. We sometimes do see kids at HHN, and we've also seen many of them crying their eyes out. The general consensus is that the event is for teens and older. So, wait until your child turns 13 and you can reexamine if they are ready.

PURCHASING DISCOUNTED TICKETS
Buy early! Universal announces Halloween Horror Nights usually six months before the event. Tickets will be cheaper as you buy them earlier with prices hiking in the late summer —and even higher after that. Also, popular dates sell out quickly (like weekends and Halloween night). The least-expensive tickets are in September through the first week of October. Weekdays are also cheaper (though HHN isn't open on every weeknight). If you are planning on visiting more than one night, season passes are also available.

Universal will often hold a promotion with Coca-Cola or another popular brand for discounted tickets on select dates. These discounts are usually listed before purchasing tickets: www.HalloweenHorrorNights.com.

Note: We have seen many people get turned away from the event or purchasing the wrong Halloween Horror Nights tickets. When visiting the website, make sure that you are purchasing tickets for Orlando and not Hollywood.

PREPARING FOR LONG LINES

The event becomes more crowded the closer to Halloween. Many times, weekday tickets (excluding Friday) don't sell out in the weeks before Halloween. Three- to five-hour-long wait times have been reported for some of the popular mazes on crowded nights. If you're planning on a crowded night, get there at the start of the event to experience the mazes before the bulk of the crowd. You can also purchase an Express Pass (usually starting around $120 extra) to skip the lines and complete them all.

EXPRESS PASS

You likely won't get to experience every maze in a single night without Express Pass. Even if you go when the sun is still out at the start of the event, it's very difficult to get through the bulk of the mazes. Every year, there are very popular mazes that have the longest lines.

We update the top choices in our free e-mail newsletter (sign up: www.magicguidebooks.com/list). Keep in mind, the daytime Express Pass will not work for HHN and hotel guest Express Passes also do not work for this event.

> **· Magic Tips ·**
> Universal sells Express Passes that work after 10pm for about half of the normal cost. To save money and time, we recommend buying one of these at the start of your night as they tend to sell out before 10pm. Look for an Express Pass distribution kiosk.

CHAPTER TWELVE

BEST-OF LISTS

INTRODUCTION

Though we do our best to condense the information in this book, we recognize that it can still feel fairly stuffed with options. To help sort through these options, we've compiled valuable lists with our most recommended experiences.

Note: We determined these lists by fun, uniqueness, and reader reviews. The food was determined by flavor, quality, uniqueness, and reader favorites.
USF = Universal Studios Florida theme park
IOA = Islands of Adventure theme park

BEST-OF LISTS

BEST RIDES AND ATTRACTIONS

1. Hagrid's Magical Creatures Motorbike Adventure (IOA)
2. Jurassic World VelociCoaster (IOA)
3. Harry Potter and the Forbidden Journey (IOA)
4. The Amazing Adventures of Spider-Man (IOA)
5. Revenge of the Mummy (USF)

6. Jurassic Park River Adventure (IOA)
7. The Incredible Hulk Coaster (IOA)
8. The Bourne Stuntacular (USF)
9. Harry Potter and the Escape from Gringotts (USF)

BEST RESTAURANTS

1. Three Broomsticks (IOA, Hogsmeade)
2. Mama Della's Ristorante (Loews Portofino Hotel)
3. Vivo Italian Kitchen (CityWalk)
4. Bubba Gump Shrimp Co. (CityWalk)
5. The Palm (Hard Rock Hotel)
6. Leaky Cauldron (USF, Diagon Alley)
7. Antojitos Authentic Mexican Food (CityWalk)
8. Thunder Falls Terrace (IOA, Jurassic Park)

BEST TREATS AND SNACKS

1. Butterbeer (USF & IOA, Butterbeer station at Diagon Alley and Hogsmeade)
2. Big Pink (USF, Lard Lad Donuts in Springfield)
3. Butterbeer Potted Cream (USF & IOA, Leaky Cauldron in Diagon Alley and Three Broomsticks in Hogsmeade)
4. Any Central Park Crepe (Central Park Crepes in Hollywood)
5. Flaming Moe [non-alcoholic] (Universal Studios, Flaming Moe's in Springfield)
6. Pumpkin Juice (Both Parks, Butterbeer station at Diagon Alley and Hogsmeade Village)
7. Any Dessert at Toothsome! (CityWalk, Toothsome Chocolate Emporium)
8. Lava Flow [alcoholic and non-alcoholic] (CityWalk, Bubba Gump's Shrimp Co.)

CHAPTER THIRTEEN

PRE-PLANNED RIDE AND ATTRACTION GUIDES

INTRODUCTION

Many visitors to the Universal Orlando Resort, are worried about not experiencing everything they want during their stay. With so many choices, it might be impossible to get everything done in one day without a plan. However, with our pre-made ride and attraction lists, you can enjoy the very best that Universal has to offer. These are *proven* to work using multiple tests over several visits. Thus, we recommend following one of our pre-made guides in order to accomplish the most on a busy day— even if you don't purchase Express Pass!

Before you get started in the Parks, make sure you complete these steps:

1. Choose one of our pre-made ride and attraction lists.
2. Get to the Park before it opens.
3. Grab a map at the entrance to help guide you around.
4. Prepare to take a break when you need to in between rides.
5. Don't rush. Keep calm, enjoy the sights, and take in the fun!

CHILD SWAP

When traveling with kids, there may be times that they cannot experience certain attractions. This could be because a child isn't tall enough to ride, or perhaps they are too scared. To remedy this, Universal Orlando uses a "Child Swap" program that allows families to experience these types of attractions without requiring the child to ride.

Child Swap works by having one adult wait with the child while the other rides. After the ride completes, the adults switch so that the other can experience it and the child is not left unaccompanied. Nearly every ride and attraction in Universal Orlando has a Child Swap. These areas are often indoors, and have televisions and things for kids to play with.

To take advantage of Child Swap, inform a Team Member near the ride that you would like to use this program. In many instances, everyone will wait through the bulk of the line until just before riding. At that time, guests will make their way to the designated Child Swap area.

· **Magic Tips** ·

If you're planning on using the Child Swap, we highly recommend using the rest of this chapter to plan out your visit. We even have a dedicated list for kids and the attractions they will likely want to experience.

ATTRACTION ASSISTANCE PASS

Universal Orlando has its own dedicated Attraction Assistance Pass, also known as AAP. Universal designed this paper pass for guests who cannot wait in conventional queues and lines. AAP works similarly to Express Pass, allowing guests and their traveling party to use a specified entrance that skips the line.

Attractions with waits of 25 minutes or less allow guests with the AAP to use the Express Pass lane to ride. However, if the line is too long, Universal may issue you a return time. Return times are issued by Team Members near the front of the attractions. You can only hold one return time, so you'll need to use or cancel with a Team Member before booking another.

Additionally, traveling parties may be limited to 4 guests per AAP. To obtain an AAP, visit Guest Relations before or after entering one of the theme parks. Universal will ask what type of assistance you need to determine if the AAP is right for you. Typically, they are accommodating to those with both visible and hidden disabilities. Passes usually expire at the end of the day, but in some instances, they can last for a few days during your visit.

· **Magic Tips** ·
Guests seeking an AAP card may have to first sign up at https://accessibilitycard.org. Universal may change their disability access, so it's important that you keep up with the latest information. To read more, visit **UniversalStudiosOrlando.com**.

VIRTUAL LINE

As a reminder, some attractions may use a virtual queue to access their lines. In some instances, this queue is the only way to access the attraction. At other times, you may see a combination of a standard line and a virtual queue used. On the day of your visit, check the Universal Orlando app to see which attractions may use this feature. We've also marked them with a "√" on our pre-planned lists.

UNIVERSAL STUDIOS FLORIDA

√ = This attraction may use the Virtual Line on the Universal Orlando app and you will need to return to the attraction later once your time is called
* = May only show seasonally

1. **Despicable Me Minion Mayhem** (Production Central)
2. **Illumination's Villain-Con Minion Blast** (Minion Land)
3. **Hollywood Rip Ride Rockit** (New York)
4. **Revenge of the Mummy** (New York)
5. **Harry Potter and the Escape from Gringotts** (Diagon Alley)
6. **Ollivanders** (Diagon Alley)
7. **Explore Diagon Alley**
8. **Fast & Furious – Supercharged** (San Francisco) √
9. **Race Through New York Starring Jimmy Fallon** (New York) √
10. **The Bourne Stuntacular** (Hollywood)
11. **E. T. Adventure** (Woody Woodpecker's Kidzone)
12. **MEN IN BLACK Alien Attack** (World's Fair)
13. **The Simpsons Ride** (Springfield)
14. **TRANSFORMERS: The Ride-3D** (New York)
15. **Universal Orlando's Cinematic Celebration** (Center Lagoon) *

In-Park Dining Recommendations:

- Leaky Cauldron (Diagon Alley)
- Central Park Crepes (Hollywood)
- Today Cafe (Production Central)

ISLANDS OF ADVENTURE

√ = This attraction may use the Virtual Line on the Universal Orlando app and you will need to return to the attraction later once your time is called
* = May only show seasonally

1. **Hagrid's Magical Creatures Motorbike Adventure** (Hogsmeade) √
2. **Harry Potter and the Forbidden Journey** (Hogsmeade)
3. **Jurassic World: VelociCoaster** (Jurassic Park)
4. **Jurassic Park River Adventure** (Jurassic Park)
5. **Raptor Encounter** (Jurassic Park)
6. **Skull Island: Reign of Kong** (Skull Island)
7. **Dudley Do-Right's Ripsaw Falls** (Toon Lagoon)
8. **Popeye & Bluto's Bilge-Rat Barges** (Toon Lagoon)
9. **Doctor Doom's Fearfall** (Marvel Super Hero Island)
10. **The Amazing Adventures of Spider-Man** (Marvel Island)
11. **The Incredible Hulk Coaster** (Marvel Island)
12. **The Cat in the Hat** (Seuss Landing)
13. **Flight of the Hippogriff** (Hogsmeade)
14. **Ollivanders** (Hogsmeade)
15. **Explore Hogsmeade Village**
16. **The Nighttime Lights at Hogwarts Castle** (Hogsmeade) *

In-Park Dining Recommendations:

- Three Broomsticks (Hogsmeade Village)
- Confisco Grille (Port of Entry)
- Fire-Eaters' Grill (The Lost Continent)

BOTH PARKS IN ONE DAY

** = You may want to skip if you don't have Express Pass
† = Extreme Coaster or Attraction
* = May only show seasonally

UNIVERSAL'S ISLANDS OF ADVENTURE

1. **Hagrid's Magical Creatures Motorbike Adventure** (Hogsmeade) √
2. **Harry Potter and the Forbidden Journey** (Hogsmeade)
3. **Jurassic World: VelociCoaster** (Jurassic Park) †
4. **Jurassic Park River Adventure** (Jurassic Park)
5. **Skull Island: Reign of Kong** (Skull Island)
6. **Dudley Do-Right's Ripsaw Falls** (Toon Lagoon)**
7. **Popeye & Bluto's Bilge-Rat Barges** (Toon Lagoon)**
8. **The Amazing Adventures of Spider-Man** (Marvel Island)
9. **Incredible Hulk Coaster** (Marvel Island) †
   Lunch: Three Broomsticks (Hogsmeade Village)
10. **Explore Hogsmeade Village** (limit to 25 minutes)
11. **Hogwarts Express** (to Universal Studios Florida)

UNIVERSAL STUDIOS FLORIDA

12. **Harry Potter and the Escape from Gringotts** (Diagon Alley)
13. **Ollivanders & Explore Diagon Alley** (limit to 25 minutes)
14. **Fast & Furious – Supercharged** (San Francisco)**
15. **Revenge of the Mummy** (New York)
16. **TRANSFORMERS: The Ride-3D** (New York)
17. **Illumination's Villain-Con Minion Blast** (Minion Land)
18. **The Bourne Stuntacular** (Hollywood)
19. **MEN IN BLACK Alien Attack** (World's Fair)
20. **The Simpsons Ride** (Springfield)
21. **Hollywood Rip Ride Rockit** (New York) †
22. **Universal Orlando's Cinematic Celebration** (Center Lagoon) *

BOTH PARKS IN ONE DAY with KIDS

*** = Great for kids 3-6

† = This attraction may be too extreme for kids under 8

UNIVERSAL'S ISLANDS OF ADVENTURE

1. **Hagrid's Magical Creatures Motorbike Adventure** (Hogsmeade) †√
2. **Harry Potter and the Forbidden Journey** (Hogsmeade) †
3. **Flight of the Hippogriff** (Hogsmeade Village)
4. **Explore Hogsmeade Village** ***
5. **Raptor Encounter** (Jurassic Park)
6. **Pteranodon Flyers** (Jurassic Park) √
7. **Dudley Do-Right's Ripsaw Falls** (Toon Lagoon) †
8. **The Amazing Adventures of Spider-Man** (Marvel Island)
9. **The Cat in the Hat** (Seuss Landing) ***
10. **The High in the Sky Seuss Trolley Train Ride** (Seuss Landing) ***
11. **Hogwarts Express** (to Universal Studios Florida) ***

UNIVERSAL STUDIOS FLORIDA

12. **Harry Potter and the Escape from Gringotts** (Diagon Alley) †
13. **Ollivanders** (Diagon Alley)
14. **Explore Diagon Alley**
15. **Jimmy Fallon's Race Through New York** (New York) √
16. **Despicable Me Minion Mayhem** (Production Central) ***
17. **Illumination's Villain-Con Minion Blast** (Minion Land)
18. **E.T. Adventure** (Woody Woodpecker's Kidzone) ***
19. **The Simpsons Ride** (Springfield)
20. **MEN IN BLACK Alien Attack** (World's Fair)
21. **Universal Orlando's Cinematic Celebration** (Center Lagoon) *

CUSTOM RIDE LIST

Park(s): ______________________________

Names: ______________ ______________

______________ ______________

______________ ______________

1. ______________________________
2. ______________________________
3. ______________________________
4. ______________________________
5. ______________________________
6. ______________________________
7. ______________________________
8. ______________________________
9. ______________________________
10. ______________________________
11. ______________________________
12. ______________________________
13. ______________________________
14. ______________________________
15. ______________________________
16. ______________________________
17. ______________________________
18. ______________________________
19. ______________________________
20. ______________________________
21. ______________________________
22. ______________________________
23. ______________________________
24. ______________________________
25. ______________________________

VACATION CHECKLIST

- ❑ Park tickets
- ❑ Ride list
- ❑ ID
- ❑ Credit card / cash
- ❑ Hotel address
- ❑ Phone (and charging cable)
- ❑ Sunscreen
- ❑ Toiletries: toothbrush, toothpaste, etc.
- ❑ Swimsuit
- ❑ Jacket
- ❑ Comfortable shoes
- ❑ Plastic bag for cellphone (water rides)
- ❑ Snacks
- ❑ Water bottles (if you aren't flying)
- ❑ Backpack or bag
- ❑ Face coverings (1 per day, if required)
- ❑ Restaurant reservations
- ❑ Universal Orlando 2024 by Magic Guidebooks
- ❑ ______________________________
- ❑ ______________________________
- ❑ ______________________________
- ❑ ______________________________
- ❑ ______________________________
- ❑ ______________________________
- ❑ ______________________________
- ❑ ______________________________
- ❑ ______________________________
- ❑ ______________________________

CONCLUSION

The Universal Orlando Resort is constantly changing, and so will this guide throughout the years. This book is our seventh edition in the series, and we want to thank you for supporting us! We hope that this guidebook is a valuable resource for your next visit!

Universal has promised to keep creating exciting experiences for years to come and announced a third theme park: Epic Universe, set to open in the Summer of 2025. This fantastic new resort area is located just south of the Endless Summer Resort and will feature new lands, attractions, dining, shopping, hotels, and more! In addition, Universal Destinations & Experiences confirmed that Super Nintendo World will open within the park. Rumors also point to more Harry Potter, Universal's Classic Monsters, How to Train Your Dragon, and other properties debuting in this new theme park. Maybe your trip is so fantastic that you'll want to return once this new park debuts!

Happy and safe travels!

Magic Guidebooks

INDEX

A

B

C

D

E

F

G

H

I

J

K

L

M

N

O

P

Q

R

S

T

U

V

W

DINING
We did not index most restaurants as they are available in alphabetical order by resort area in the Dining Guide chapter.

Was our guide helpful?

★★★★★

If so, please leave us a quick review telling other customers what you found useful on Amazon.com. Your reviews GREATLY help us out!

Wishing you a magical vacation!
Magic Guidebooks

Printed in Great Britain
by Amazon

34183381R00115